SWIM WITH THE SHARKS

OUTSMART THE MARKET

Simple Rules | Proven Investment Strategies | Unlimited Profits

TOMMY TURNER

Swim with the Sharks
Outsmart The Market

ISBNs
978-1-954269-00-2 (paperback)
978-1-954269-01-9 (hardback)
978-1-954269-02-6 (eBook)

Acknowledgments

This book is dedicated to my mom and dad, who worked so hard to give me a good home and a loving upbringing. I wish they were still alive to see all the blessings that I have come to enjoy in my life.

My children and grandchildren are undoubtably the greatest blessings in my life. No matter the amount of money I will ever make trading stocks or any other successes I might experience in life will ever compare to the love and joy I have in my family and friends.

Legal Notice or Disclaimer

This book is not intended to be used as financial advice. Any of the stocks and/or techniques and examples mentioned and/or investing ideas discussed in this book are strictly for illustration purposes only and should in no way be taken as financial advice. Investing in stocks is **very risky**! You should do considerable study and research prior to using any real money to invest in any stock.

Contents

Introduction

As I began to write this book, I had not yet determined all of the details such as what the title or subtitle would be nor did I know what catchy phrases or other aspects might go on the cover and influence the final book design. What I did know was that it would all take shape by the time I finished writing this book. As I start this first paragraph, all the elements are still a mystery yet to unfold. Whatever the case may be, by the time you hold this book in your hand to read this material, all of those details will have sorted themselves out.

So, what is the point of my even mentioning this tidbit of information about not knowing all the elements like the title, the subtitle or book cover design at the very beginning? Quite simply, it's because that not knowing is exactly how the stock market is every trading day. The "details, main features, and book design" of each trading day have yet to be determined until the final bell of each trading day.

The title is always the same: *Welcome to the Stock Exchange*. The plot is always the same: a series of ups and downs as news comes and goes throughout the day while the bulls and bears battle for position. However, many details and design aspects of each trading day will always be somewhat of a mystery right up until the very last trade of the day.

Some trading days can best be described as *A Nightmare on Wall Street.* They start out bad and often end much worse. Then other days in the market are all rainbows and pots of gold. On some days, the market is rather boring; other days it is a total rush, changing its design by the minute—right up until the very end.

Now, you might say, "Well, if the market is up BIG in the pre-market and everything is mostly green, then we pretty much know it's going to be a good green day for the bulls. We can get a head start on creating the heading and design for that day."

Well, yes, that plan is certainly possible, but there are no guarantees. If you play the stock market game for long at all, you will see some crazy reversals in either direction. Just when you think you know what is going to happen next, the exact opposite happens.

I have witnessed days where the overall market stayed green all day long right up until the last 30 minutes or so of the trading day, and then almost like a storm moving in, within minutes a dark ominous cloud formed over the market. Stocks sold off rapidly, and everything turned red to close. If you had already created the title and book design for that trading day, you would need to scrap it and start all over.

However, I believe that unpredictability and the fascination of a new design every day is what creates the intrigue and drive for most stock traders to return day after day to play the stock market trading game. Most retail traders have a love-hate relationship with the market at times. I liken the affiliation to a golfer who continually goes back out to the golf course in hopes of a better day—even after a horrible round of golf the previous day. The retail stock trader makes his best attempt to conquer the market again and again as well.

When I first started gathering the material and assembling my thoughts for this book, I was very excited as I had been longing to delve into my fascination and passion for investing and trading stocks for some time. However, I had felt the timing was just not right until now.

I wish that everyone could experience the incredible successes and joys that I have come to know through trading and investing in the stock market over the last several years. However, as I thought more about my message and how I would teach others to make money by investing and trading stocks, I felt a "check" in my spirit.

I was reminded that I must always seek the Lord first and rely on the wisdom of the Holy Spirit in ALL that I do. This pursuit of and reliance on the Lord is especially true when it comes to investing my hard-earned money in the stock market.

I believe you must follow two extremely valuable principles when it involves money—if you truly want to be successful.

Principle One

You must **always** recognize that no amount of money will ever make you truly happy or replace the love and forgiveness of the Lord or the love of others in your life. When you accept Jesus into your life and learn to value relationship with the Lord and others more than money, you will discover blessings and joy that money simply cannot buy.

Principle Two

Be a generous giver of your finances! You will have plenty of money to enjoy a wonderful life when you are a generous giver of your finances. I have discovered that you simply cannot outgive God. The more I am able to freely give of my finances, the more it seems He blesses me.

I want to caution you though. You do not want to develop an attitude of giving in order to receive. Once you learn to release your finances freely and give generously out of obedience, trusting that the Lord will supply all of your need according to His riches in glory, then you are in a position for blessing.

> *But my God shall supply all your need according to his riches in glory by Christ Jesus.*
>
> —Philippians 4:19 King James Version

I also believe you must observe two valuable keys when it comes to investing and trading stocks. These two keys are so vitally important that I have adapted them into my trading rules as well. You will read all about these powerful trading rules and more as we progress through the pages of this book.

Key One

Stay in the **neutral** zone with each investment and/or trade. An old Wall Street saying is that "financial markets are driven by two powerful emotions: GREED and FEAR. The fact is, you will make money at times, and you will also lose money at times. Stocks will go up, and stocks will go down. They always have, and they always will.

Whenever you are "wandering" too far outside of the neutral zone, you are either leaning too far left and feeling fearful or too far right and becoming greedy. When you sense that you've entered the zone of fear or greed, then it's time to return to the neutral zone.

Key Two

You must keep a Positive Winning Mindset. This type of mindset goes beyond simply believing you will win at the stock market trading game and make money. In fact, this mindset is built by following a simple set of trading rules as you'll discover in the pages of this book. It is important to note that a positive winning mindset can also be influenced when losing money as well.

Far too often when you are losing money on a trade, right after you bail out and sell the stock, it will seemingly pop right back up. That outcome can play with a person's mind—especially when you witness it firsthand a few times. It almost seems as if the entire stock market was waiting for YOU to sell your shares before it poured out the reward.

Well, I hate to burst your bubble, but the stock market really does not care who, what, when, where or why you buy or sell a stock. The reason you bought and/or sold at seemingly the wrong time was simply because you allowed your emotions to get outside the neutral zone and feed into the price movement and/or the news or a myriad of other influencing factors. So, you need to learn to stay in the neutral zone and hang tough with a disciplined set of trading rules in order to develop and maintain a positive winning mindset.

Investing and trading stocks in the stock market can be a thrill much like you might experience on a rollercoaster ride. Ironically, the last book I wrote in my popular *Quick Charge Your Life* series was on learning how to crush panic attacks and calm anxiety. I mention that book because I have experienced many anxiety attacks and panic over the years as an active stock trader, but the joy and satisfaction that I receive from trading and investing in stocks has become one of those rushes I live for whether it be an exciting rush when I am making money or an intense rush when I am losing money. Either way, I absolutely love the rush and challenges of this stock market rollercoaster ride when trading stocks!

The key is that I have discovered how to **handle** the emotional rollercoaster ride filled with many ups and downs that come with trading stocks. I will also teach you how to handle your emotions when you're riding on the stock market rollercoaster. I want to draw your attention to the fact that I said **handle** the rollercoaster ride and **not** how to **avoid** the rollercoaster.

Every stock trader must stand in line just like all the other stock traders in the world and hand their tickets to the Wall Street Ride attendant each morning in order to get back on the stock market rollercoaster when the market officially opens. However, by following some simple trading rules and other powerful concepts presented in this book, you can discover how to enjoy the ride and not be influenced by the market's ups, downs, twist and turns.

I will be using some basic stock trading lingo and/or terms like "stop loss" or "swing trade," etc., assuming that most people reading this book have already read other books on stock trading, watched videos or purchased courses on investing and trading stocks. Having some familiarity with the terms I will be using will be helpful. However, even if you haven't a rudimentary knowledge, I will keep my principles and tips simple and understandable. If you do happen to come across any terms in this book that I may use such as "shorting a stock" or creating proper "stop losses" and any other unfamiliar terms, I would recommend your doing some quick research online. You will easily find all the information you need on any of the simple, but unfamiliar, trading terms I might use in this book.

Before we get too far into this material, I want to strongly emphasize that stock trading and investing is not for everyone. Anything that I share in this book is simply based on my personal experiences, opinions and/or information that I have learned along the way from my own stock trading and investing experiences over nearly 37 years and counting. Anything I share in this book should in no way be considered as financial advice. When it comes to investing and trading stocks, you are 100 percent responsible for all of your own actions, decisions, gains and losses.

I can tell you that I have had wonderful success in my trading and investing career, but I have also had many failures and roadblocks along the way as well. You'll read about both the good and the bad. I consider myself to be one of the few who is blessed enough to say that I actually make good money trading and investing in stocks. I hope the pages ahead will help you discover the same blessings as well one day.

> *"The stock market is filled with individuals who know the price of everything, but the value of nothing."*
>
> —Phillip Fisher

CHAPTER 1
Where It All Began

Since this chapter is about beginnings, I want to first emphasize the importance of reading through the introduction of this book before diving into this first chapter. Far too often we tend to skip the introduction, acknowledgments, and other front material in a book, but the introduction really helps set the tone for the entire book. If you happened to skip the introduction, please go back now and read it before you begin this chapter.

Now for the *Beginning...*

I can still remember the beginning of my journey and passion for trading and investing in stocks like it was yesterday, but my journey actually began in 1983. Just to put this time frame into perspective as to how long ago 1983 really was...I started trading and investing before smartphones, Google, Facebook, Amazon, eBay, and so many other advancements and companies that we use and rely on so heavily in our world today. Just imagine a world without Google, Netflix, Facebook, YouTube, and Amazon... As you can see, I started investing and trading stocks in a much simpler world a long time ago...

Thinking of all that has changed in my life and in this world even since my very first stock trade in 1983 is utterly amazing. That first stock trade really came about quite by total accident. Perhaps, though, it was through coincidence or even divine direction that I started in this wonderful and fascinating business of investing and trading stocks.

At the time I was living with my late sister, Sharlene, in Redmond, Washington. A timely phone call began to shape my investing life and form some of the material for the pages of the book that you have begun reading. I can still recall exactly where I was when a misdirected, but very intriguing, phone call came. I had just walked out of an upstairs bedroom and headed down the hallway when I heard the phone ring.

When I answered, the gentleman on the other end of the line asked for "Tom Turner."

I said, "Yes, this is Tom."

The caller sounded somewhat confused, so he inquired again, "Is Tom Turner there?"

Again, I answered, "Yes, this is Tom Turner. How can I help you?"

He still sounded puzzled but continued on, saying, "Tom, this is your stockbroker with so-and-so company," and without taking a breather, he said, "I have a great stock investment to share with you, and…"

I realized this caller was actually trying to reach my dad, Tom Turner, Sr. It so happened that my parents often parked their motorhome on my sister's property, so they would use her phone number for contact. After all, in 1983 no cell phones were available to the public.

I stopped him in mid-sentence and said, "I'm sorry, but I believe you're trying to reach my dad, Tom Turner, Sr."

He chuckled then and said, "I thought you sounded somewhat younger than I recalled from our last phone conversation."

"My dad is not in, but I have some extra money to invest. I would love to learn more about this stock investment idea and also about stock investing in general."

As a result of that phone conversation, we set up an appointment for later that week to meet at his office. When I arrived at the brokerage firm in downtown Bellevue, I distinctly remember walking into the brokerage office and witnessing several stockbrokers all sitting at their desks busily calling and talking on the phone. Looking around, I thought I was on a movie set!

I'm sure the brokers were all calling clients to tell them about exciting investment opportunities just like this broker must have been doing the day he was trying to reach my dad. Fortunately for me, I intercepted the phone call, and, at that time, the material for this book slowly began to take form. However, I had no idea in 1983 that I would even become a published author one day—let alone write a book on trading and investing in stocks.

After I sat down in a chair in front of his desk, this broker proceeded to tell me all about a sports shoe and apparel company that had started trading publicly in December of 1980, and the stock was really on the rise. Perhaps you have heard of the sports shoe and apparel company he was referring to—Nike.

In 1983, I did not know much, if anything, about buying and selling stocks, and I surely did not know about the possibilities of owning stock in a company such as Nike. He explained that by purchasing and owning stock in a company like Nike, I was basically a partner on a small scale in the company by sharing in a portion of the company's successes and/or failures.

> *"Although it's easy to forget sometimes, a share is not a lottery ticket...it's part ownership of a business."*
>
> —Peter Lynch

I did know all about the popularity of Nike shoes, and I may have even worn a pair of Nike shoes to his office for my appointment. However, I did not know a person could buy stock in the company itself. Come to think of it, I do remember seeing an old college picture of my friends and me sitting in a dorm room, and I was wearing a pair of Nike shoes. Even owning a pair of those older classic Nike shoes in pristine condition now would be worth a small fortune! *Maybe I better go dig through my closet and see if I still have them!*

Anyway, this stockbroker told me that he felt Nike was primed to be an excellent stock investment, and one that I should consider owning for a long time. Based on his encouragement, I told him to put in an order to purchase 100 shares of Nike (stock symbol NKE), and my investing career was off and running...

After I bought those 100 shares, I would go down to the local convenience store every week to purchase a *Wall Street Journal* or a *USA Today* newspaper. Then I would scroll through the stock symbols to find NKE and check to see if the shares had gone up or down in price. A month or so later, the stock had jumped considerably. *Wow! I can't believe how easy this stock investing thing is,* I thought. *You just buy a stock, it goes up, and you're making money—without really doing anything!*

I certainly wish I could tell you that it really was that easy, but investing takes more than that. I also wish I could tell you that I kept those 100 shares of Nike stock for many years like the broker advised. However, back then I did not listen to that stockbroker's advice about holding this particular stock long term.

Hey, I was only a 23-year-old kid and seeing that increase in my account was just so cool that I decided to have him sell my 100 shares of NKE and take my winnings. I think I made about one thousand dollars in four or five weeks, and that was after the brokers' commissions. Man, that win felt great! Remember, this was back in 1983 so $1,000 was a sizable amount of money to a 23-year-old. Come to think of it, a thousand dollars is still a lot of money for a 23-year-old today...

I was HOOKED with this stock investing stuff. However, if only I had just kept my initial 100 share investment in Nike (NKE) like he suggested way back then and held it until now. I would have thousands of shares simply due to several stock splits, but that's a whole different story.

I truly don't regret selling that stock because I have had the good fortune of doing very well with my investing and trading career thus far, and that initial phone call from a random stock broker, and then the subsequent winning trade in Nike (NKE) started it all for me...

After that initial investment, I continued to buy and sell a few more stocks through this broker for another few months or so, but then life eventually moved on. I got away from investing in stocks for several years.

I'll admit, I did not make too much money trying to buy and sell stocks with the high commissions you had to pay back then for a stock broker to execute the transactions. The large commission fees would eat up a big chunk of my profits. I am sure my stockbroker was happy that I made so many trades, but looking back on it now I realize it was not a very smart strategy.

In 1987 I started a career in the piano tuning and sales industry. Although I had a busy new career and stopped actively trading stocks, my interest and intrigue for stock trading never wavered. Through the years I would continue to watch the stock market by picking up a *Wall Street Journal* or browse through a *USA Today* newspaper whenever I got my hands on one at the newsstand. (There was no Internet available to me back then, so you had to make do with what was available).

Then something wonderful happened in the 1990s. First, the Internet was becoming the rage by the mid-90s, so I finally got a dial-up Internet account around 1995. The convenience of having my own personal Internet access allowed me the luxury to do research right from my home on any stock price or find other information on a stock that I was interested in following.

Soon after I got my dial-up Internet account, I went down to my local brokerage office and opened an account. My stockbroker would suggest a stock or two to watch, I would go home and do my research online, then we would put together a trade plan. This went fairly well for a couple of years, but again, the high brokerage fees made it difficult to make much profit as a trader.

However, more advancements were on the way which made things much better for investing... Around 1998 my cable company started promoting highspeed Internet or at least it was highspeed for back then. The 1998 version was much faster than the dial-up connection I had been using, but it was nothing compared to the highspeed Internet speeds we have access to today! So, I upgraded my Internet account to highspeed, and my stock trading life was changed forever!

Soon after getting the highspeed Internet account, I opened an online brokerage account through Scottrade, and I was able to make my own stock trades right from the comfort of my home for only seven dollars per transaction. When I first opened my online trading account, I still had my other brokerage account as well. So, I would still get stock advice through my stockbroker and buy a few shares through him, but I would also initiate a small position on my own through my online Scottrade account as well.

Once again, one of my first initial investments when getting started with trading stocks online was a home run. I bought stock in a company called eBay (EBAY). I'm sure most of you reading this book have heard of this online auction company as well. My eBay stock soared almost as soon as I bought it, so I quickly sold my shares and made a very nice profit around $2000 at the time.

Again, I could not believe how easy this stock trading business was... So, soon after this win, I decided to close my other brokerage account and told my stockbroker that I was going to take all my money and start trading exclusively online through Scottrade and make my own trades.

Needless to say, I don't think he was too happy, and perhaps he was even a bit concerned about my decision to go it alone. I am sure many stockbrokers back then questioned a person's decision to trade online, and they likely were not happy with all the options that were rapidly becoming available to anyone who had a little money and an Internet connection. Online brokerage firms opened the door for many who wanted to take investing matters into their own hands to buy and sell stocks right from their own homes or offices.

I was so excited that I now had the ability to research and purchase stocks online without having to pay a broker those outrageous commissions. I had the ability to keep an eye on the market news, watch stock charts, buy and sell stocks online—all from my own home office for only $7 per trade. Life just couldn't get any better, or could it?

However, the fact is, I did not have a good set of rules to follow or any discipline developed for trading and investing in stocks back then, so I still never really made any money in the early days of my online trading career either (even with lower commissions and transaction fees). Still, being in the market was a total rush, and I LOVED the challenge. I was very determined that I would eventually figure out how to win at this stock trading game!

Unfortunately, in the early days of my online trading career, every time I would find a winning stock trade or two, I seemed to have this uncanny ability to always pick a loser or two and give back most if not all of my winnings and more. Sadly, that is the story for 90 percent of those out there today who are trying to make money buying and selling stocks online.

Like so many who search for the secret to making money trading stocks, I also purchased several books on how to read stock charts and how to evaluate a company, and just about every other course or book I could find at the time on stock trading and investing. I would study for hours on end, searching for the million-dollar solution to making money by trading stocks, but I had little success.

Later on, I subscribed to a few stock services that would suggest stock picks, and I did fairly well for a while based on their stock picks, but again, I seemed to always find myself back at zero profit or even losing money each year. However, the losses never seemed to discourage me as I just loved crunching the numbers and taking on the challenges of figuring out a system to conquer the market. Yes, stock trading and investing was exhilarating, and the drive for success was in my blood.

In one book that I read, I learned about a trading strategy called "swing trading" where you would buy a stock and hold it for a few weeks up to couple months or so in hopes of catching a run up or down, depending on how you played it long or short. I had already been using this same type of stock trading technique for a few years, but I did not know that there was actually a name for this style of trading stocks.

I loved the concept of the swing trade strategy, so I focused most of my attention on learning more about this strategy. We will delve deeper into this strategy in the pages ahead, but I can promise you that what I teach is not what you've read before. I have an edge to winning that I will share with you in the pages of this book.

Another popular method of trading is called "day trading," but I strongly urge you to avoid this method of trading until you have a sizable account to work with and are very familiar with the risk involved. However, for those who have more funds and may want to try day trading at some point, I do have a very unique strategy that I use to day trade that I will share later in the book as well.

I feel you can probably relate a winning stock trade to the same feeling gold miners must get when they are struck by the "Gold bug." Once you choose a few winning stock trades, the desire to win gets in your blood; you want to do it again and again. This very passion and excitement continually urged me on to read more books, watch videos, and study everything I could get my hands on to become a better stock trader and investor.

As most of you may know if you've read any of my *Quick Charge Your Life* books, my life really started to take some major positive adjustments starting around 2014. That is when I was given the opportunity to manage a piano store. Since I had spent nearly 35 years and counting in the piano business, this opportunity was a perfect fit for me and gave me considerably more income. Thus, I had the wherewithal to invest even more money into the stock market. However, not until 2017 did things really start to turn around in my life as I shared in my first book simply titled *Quick Charge Your Life.*

I did not share too much about my stock trading and investing career in my *Quick Charge* series books that I wrote because my positive winning mindset, trading rules, and trading methods were all being refined into simple-to-follow principles and rules that I could explain and teach others.

I am sure somewhere hidden in the back of my mind, there was always a plan for this book, but it was not until I really started realizing tremendous success in my personal life, business life, and especially in my stock trading and investing career that I knew I had to formulate a system for my stock trading methods and release them in a book. I could explain my simple-to-follow set of rules and then coach others so they can experience success in life, as well as in trading stocks.

Yes, although I had not really thought of this particular book when I first started writing books, I'm not surprised that my passion and intrigue for investing and trading stocks has led me to write a book specifically on this topic now. Perhaps I'll write even more books on stock trading and investing in the future... My desire and hope is to help as many people as I can to live the *Quick Charge Concept* and find financial freedom through investing and trading stocks as I have enjoyed.

As I have already mentioned, I have read many books, watched several videos, and purchased a few stock subscriptions services over the years to learn all that I can about this fascinating and challenging world of stock trading and investing. Many of the books, services, and systems that I have studied were good, but the practices that I have found to be the most successful and beneficial for stock trading and investing was not something I discovered in any of those books or videos.

You might be wondering, *So what did you learn or discover that I need to know?*

Well, the first truth I learned was not directly related to stock investing at all. I must continually stick to the principles that I use for living the *Quick Charge Concept.* Living by these principles have, in turn, led me to develop a disciplined set of trading rules and a trading plan to maintain a positive winning mindset for investing and trading stocks.

If you've read any of my *Quick Charge* books, then inevitably you've heard about the *Quick Charge Concept.* I would be remiss not to include a quick overview of this principle here. The *Quick Charge Concept* is about the following:

- It's about developing a personal relationship with the Lord and continually seeking Him to energize you with His power.

- It's about taking responsibility for your happiness by thinking positive thoughts—no matter what you may encounter in life.
- It's about learning to be calm and trusting the Lord during the storms in your life.
- It's about finding joy and blessing when you inspire others.
- It's also about generously giving of all that God has given you.

In a nutshell, the *Quick Charge Concept* is an invitation for you to intentionally, deliberately and consciously change the way you think so that you might discover all the *quick-charge* outlets with which God surrounds you every single day of your life. The *quick-charge concept* will allow you to continually charge the power already within you to move past your perceived limitations and boldly step into the life you were born to create. Learn it, live it, and inspire others...*Quick Charge Your Life!*

As I have already mentioned, some of the books I have read and/or stock services I have subscribed to on stock investing and trading have been helpful along my stock trading journey, but living out the *Quick Charge Concept,* learning to stay in the neutral zone by controlling my emotions and developing a positive winning mindset have been the biggest factors to my success in trading and investing in stocks hands down.

> *"I will tell you how to become rich. Close the doors. Be fearful when others are greedy. Be greedy when others are fearful."*
>
> —Warren Buffett

> *"In investing, what is comfortable is rarely profitable."*
>
> —Robert Arnott

CHAPTER 2

Paper Trade or Real Money?

If you have ever read or studied anything about investing and/or trading stocks, then I am certain that one of the most common themes or suggestions you may have heard when it comes to getting started is to start out by using a "paper trade" account.

Whether or not you are familiar with the concept of a paper trade account, please stay with me. I want to quickly explain what a paper trade account is for those who may not know. For this chapter, understanding the concept is important to the overall content in this chapter. Most online brokerage firms will allow investors to set up a paper trade account on their trading platform. Basically, using a paper account is like using virtual Monopoly game money for buying and selling stocks instead of using your own "real" money. Of course, since it is only "play" money, you cannot lose or gain any REAL money...*if only investing were really that easy!*

The idea behind starting with a paper trade account is to familiarize the trader with trading stocks and managing a portfolio without risking his own "real" money. Though a great concept for total beginners, the paper trade account is NOT the best way to learn how to build a portfolio for those who are already familiar with buying and selling stocks. Definitely, it is not how to learn to build a positive winning mindset for stock trading success.

I personally feel that some of the reasoning or logic behind the idea of paper trading is somewhat flawed, and this chapter will eventually explain my reasoning. The concept behind using paper trading is to gain confidence in managing your trades and money without risking your own real money. When you feel you have gained a good grasp of how to manage your portfolio, then you can start using your own **real** money account to trade and invest in stocks.

I find this concept of paper trading flawed in that most people will be deceived into thinking they are trading experts or possibly even stock trading geniuses if they are able to double or triple their paper trade account by making some stunning stock picks and aggressive trades. However, until you are using your own REAL money, you are never able to truly manage your **emotions**. From my standpoint, learning to manage your emotions and developing a positive winning mindset constitutes 97 percent of winning the game when it comes to any real success in trading stocks.

Trust me, I have read book after book on how to read charts. I have subscribed to several stock picking services. I have read books and watched videos on how to choose a good company and how to read profit and loss statements, etc. I would be the first to say that many good services and books are available, but if I've said it once, I'll say it again based on personal experience, I can tell you that when you learn to stay in the neutral zone, better control your emotions, and adhere to a solid set of trading rules to help you form a positive winning mindset, you will become a much better trader and investor, period!

Certainly, I do NOT think anyone can ever fully master ALL of their thoughts and emotions when it comes to making money and especially when losing money in the stock market, but you

WILL learn to manage those thoughts and emotions more efficiently in order to win in the stock trading game. If you can remember anything from this book, please take these next two statements and affix them firmly into your mind.

> **Statement One**
> Based on personal experience, I can tell you that when you learn to stay in the neutral zone, better control your emotions, and adhere to a solid set of trading rules to help you form a positive winning mindset, you will become a much better trader and investor.
>
> **Statement Two**
> I do NOT think anyone can ever fully master ALL of their thoughts and emotions when it comes to making money or especially when losing money in the stock market. You WILL learn to manage those thoughts and emotions more efficiently in order to win in the stock trading game!

I purposely included a "hidden" message with three capitalized words in the second statement that I want to call attention to: **NOT ALL WILL**. The explanation should be very clear, for they mean exactly that!

Not everyone will learn to stay in the neutral zone and manage their emotions or stay disciplined enough to follow a solid set of trading rules to develop a positive winning mindset in order to win at this stock trading game. The statistics are rather daunting; nearly 90 percent of the people who try their hand at investing never make any money trading and investing in stocks!

Millions of people swim around in the stock market pool, giving away all their money to the hungry sharks of the trading world. My purpose in writing this book is not to teach anyone how to become a big trading shark making millions of dollars per year. However, I do believe the trading rules and principles revealed in this book will teach you how to swim confidently with the sharks in order to make a very nice return on your money—if you're disciplined to follow them!

And back to trading with a paper trade account...

When it comes to paper trading, I do feel that one aspect is extremely beneficial ONLY in the following cases. If you have never traded stocks before or if you are new to a certain trading platform offered by the online broker you are using, I feel paper trading is possibly the best way to learn when it comes to buying and selling stocks.

One other possible benefit to paper trading is perhaps the ability to learn how to set different types of stop losses and/or execute various buy and sell orders rather than make costly mistakes with your own real money. However, once you are familiar with how to buy and sell stocks on the platform you are using and understand the various types of stops and buy orders, then I feel it is best to dive in and start using your own REAL money to learn how to trade stocks. However, there is a method to my madness!

Now, let's talk about REAL money...

The number 100 is a common number when it comes to buying and/or selling stocks. Stocks are typically bought and sold in lots of 100 shares, but that commonality does not necessarily mean a person must or even should buy in lots of 100, 200, 500 or 1000 shares, etc... My suggestion is to start slow and purchase only a few shares. Since you will be using your own real money, if you only buy two to five shares, you are not risking nearly as much money as if you were to buy 100 or 200 shares or more.

You've likely heard the saying *"A penny saved is a penny earned."*

Well, it's better to make only a few dollars or more importantly only lose a few dollars as you learn, but never forget you are still working with REAL money. I want to illustrate what a small stock purchase with real money looks like.

Let's say you purchased 2 shares of XYZ stock priced at $100 per share. You are risking all $200. 2 shares x $100 per share = $200 invested.

Now, when I say you're risking **all** $200, I am assuming the worst possible case scenario in that shortly after you purchased the stock, the company would go belly up and disappear off the face of the earth. The stock would be deemed worthless. Obviously, this scenario is highly unlikely when purchasing a quality stock, but for the purpose of this illustration, let's assume the possibility is there. In essence, you are risking **all** $200.

When trading stocks that are priced in the $100 and above price range, it is not uncommon for many of the stocks in this price range to move 5% to 10% or even much more in a few days to a couple weeks, whether that be up or down in price or even in both directions.

Let's look at what can happen when purchasing 2 shares of XYZ stock at a price of $100 per share, and then the stock goes up 8% in the next month. That means the stock price would have increased to $108 per share, which also means an increase of $16 in gain.

$8 per share increase x 2 shares owned = $16 gain

I know this gain does not sound like much. Imagine if you would have purchased 100 shares! If you would have purchased 100 shares, then doing the math means 100 shares x $8 increase per share = $800 in gain.

I already know that you're thinking: an $800 gain sure sounds much more appealing than $16! However, what if the scenario were reversed?

What if you had purchased 2 shares of XYZ stock at $100 per share, but a few weeks later, the stock dropped 8% in value? That would mean the stock price is now trading at $92 per share.

$8 per share decrease in value x 2 shares owned = -$16 loss

If you look at the larger purchase of 100 shares x -$8 per share = -$800 in loss.

That $16 gain or loss does not make that smaller purchase look so bad when computing the possible comparison, does it?

By using smaller trade amounts while you learn, you are still using your own real money, and you can get a sense of what it feels like to manage REAL money. Indeed, you are not taking on the huge risk of losing hundreds or even thousands of dollars if you had invested even more real money.

I know I said you are risking ALL $200 even when purchasing only 2 shares, but again, that was only to keep the example real, as there is never a 100-percent guarantee that any stock will hold up. However, chances are relatively good that a company with a $100 share price will be reasonably solid and not go out of business a day or two later. The possibility is very real that the company or stock market could crumble overnight, so any money you invest in a stock is always at risk of disappearing.

There are two hidden benefits to learning by using small amounts of money as well, and they can sneak up on you. They are important elements regarding what this book is all about.

The first hidden benefit is when you initiate a small position using REAL money, and the stock suddenly gaps up a large percentage. This sudden gap up can create a rather bittersweet feeling. On the one hand, you are happy that you made the right call and made some money. However, on the other hand, you entertain that **sick feeling** in your gut when you weigh the fact that you could have made SO MUCH MORE MONEY if you had only bought 100 shares or more—like your gut instincts were telling you to buy. The emotions can alternate between positive and negative—blissful to gloomy.

However, this scenario presents an opportunity for you to practice keeping your emotions in check and staying in the neutral zone. Learn to be grateful that you still made the right call and made some decent profits. Do not be disappointed that you did not make as much as you would have if only you had listened to your gut instincts and purchased more shares.

The second hidden benefit that sneaks up on you is the **discipline** you will develop by staying patient and sticking to a good trading plan and a solid set of rules. When you discipline yourself to trade in small amounts for an adequate period of time, you really learn how to manage your emotions and money well. Learning this discipline can be a huge benefit later on!

I promise, this experience will prove to be invaluable to your trading success down the road. I still make small trades even to this very day just to keep myself grounded and aligned with my trading rules and philosophies.

Once again, I will substantially address the need to develop a positive winning mindset and managing your emotions to stay in the neutral zone. Therefore, I encourage you to start out by trading small numbers of shares using REAL money to teach you how to trade and give you plenty of practice. Following this plan will also help you learn how to manage your emotions when a stock goes up big or when it falls hard.

Remember, it is always extremely important to pay very close attention to your thoughts and emotions when you look at your smaller investment portfolio and see that a stock just went up 15%, 20% or more in a short period of time and also when it drops 15% or more in a short period of time.

Always learn to check your emotions and balance those feelings into the neutral zone. Try to stay in the middle of your emotions. Visualize a meter with a needle and keep that needle in the middle or neutral zone...don't allow the emotional needle to go too far left or too far right. In other words, do not become too upset or troubled over the lack of gains you could have had if only you would have listened to your gut and invested more. You must resist those feelings of greed when you have thoughts that you will follow your gut next time and invest a much larger amount rather than be disciplined to build your portfolio slowly.

Side Note: Of importance to mention is that this method of buying in small lots has become possible and much more cost effective because many online brokerage firms have now dropped their commissions to $0—ZERO. You can now buy and sell shares without paying any commission fees with many online brokers.

As I am writing this book, the zero $0 commissions are a relatively new development. I used to pay about $7 per transaction. Once I reached a certain account level, they lowered my commission fees to $4.95 per trade, but ZERO commissions are obviously a much better fee!

The $7 commission fee that used to be charged was still much lower than the old days of paying a broker to buy and sell stocks for you. Now that online brokerage companies compete against each other, many have eliminated their commissions. These zero commissions make it possible for the average retail investor to buy and sell in small lots since they are not incurring fees for every single trade, which added up quickly. **End of side note...**

Learn to stay focused on the task at hand, which is to remain in the neutral zone with your emotions whether it be a good trade and or a bad trade. In the end that is all it is—just trades of money in stocks based on the thought it will go up or go down, depending on the direction you have played the stock—long or short.

One day you'll hopefully be working with thousands of dollars and then tens of thousands of dollars. If you are one of the blessed few, perhaps you'll be trading with hundreds of thousands or even millions of REAL dollars...

Yes, it is VERY possible, and I can tell you from personal experience that starting with a small account balance and slowly building it into an incredible REAL MONEY portfolio balance is amazing! I'm living proof it is possible, and if I can do it, anyone can do it.

> *"The four most dangerous words in investing are: "This time it's different."*
>
> —Sir John Templeton

> *"Wide diversification is only required when investors do not understand what they are doing."*
>
> —Warren Buffett

CHAPTER 3

Choose Winning Stocks

A few years ago, I developed some basic guidelines or tips to find good stocks to watch for potential winning trades that have continued to work very well for me. I am more than happy to share that information with you in this chapter.

I should mention that my preferred method of trading stocks is to swing trade stocks. I only day trade on occasion. When following the steps outlined in this chapter for choosing stocks to watch for winning trades, I am mainly looking for stocks to watch for potential swing trade candidates.

Tip Number One

Choose stocks that you are knowledgeable about. What do I mean? Choose stocks associated with companies and products or services that you know and use. We all have products or services that we use and companies we know and possibly shop at every week. It's likely that many of these companies are publicly traded on the stock exchange.

The following are a few of these companies: McDonald's (MCD), Walmart (WMT), NIKE (NKE), Microsoft (MSFT),

Amazon (AMZN), Dollar General (DG), Dollar Tree (DLTR), AT&T (T), Coke (COKE), Pepsi (PEP), Verizon (VZ), and so forth,

Perhaps there is a franchise business in your area that you would love to own if only you had the money. Well, if that franchise is a publicly traded company on the stock exchange, then you can own a small piece of the pie by owning that company's stock.

Tip Number Two

Stick to stocks that have a stock price of at least $10 dollars or more per share and preferably even higher. I am not a fan of buying penny stocks or low-cost, high-risk stocks. I will admit that buying a few speculative $5 stocks or low-cost penny stocks is fine—as long as you are only using a very small portion of your portfolio funds. For the most part, I do not recommend that you spend much time focusing on low-cost stocks.

I realize you can purchase several more shares of a 50¢ or $1 stock versus a $10 stock or even a $100 stock, but I would not risk an abundance of funds in these penny stocks. I have found the better investment is almost always to go with the higher-priced quality stocks.

Yes, there is always a possibility that one of your 50¢ stock picks might skyrocket and make you a fortune, but the odds are not in your favor. However, if you allocate a very small portion of your portfolio to penny stocks and get lucky, then great!

Tip Number Three

Choose stocks that have a daily volume of at least 500,000 shares or more traded, and preferably, one million or more shares traded per day. This tip is not always a hard set-in-stone rule. However, I tend to find that stocks with higher daily volume have a better chance of consistent movement if you are looking for stocks to swing trade.

Tip Number Four

Look for stocks with dividends. This tip mainly applies more for those interested in longer term investing, but there are times when I will swing trade a stock that I also plan to hold some shares longer term for investment purposes. I prefer trading stocks with some sort of dividend even if it is a very small dividend. However, I do trade several stocks that do not have a dividend. I will address building a portfolio of longer-term growth and dividend investment portfolios later in the book.

Tip Number Five

Before investing into any stock for swing trading purposes, check to see when the company will report earnings. I like to study a stock through at least one earnings report to see how the company reacts. This information also gives me a current status on the health of the company.

When swing trading, I tend to avoid holding a trade through an earnings announcement. However, I will often buy a stock a few weeks before earnings and sell it just prior to the close of market on the earnings day if earnings will be announced after the market close. However, if the announcement will come in the morning, then I will sell the day before the earnings call. Of course, you could buy a stock and see a huge run up in your favor after the earnings announcement, but in most cases, it is often a riskier play for the smaller retail investor to hold through earnings.

The main point is always to wait and study the stock through at least one earnings report to get a sense of how the stock is doing. Also, pay close attention as to how the price action is for the stock leading up to the earnings announcement.

Tip Number Six

Check the 52-week high and low to see where the stock is currently trading. If it's at its very low or very highest point, then do some further research to see what has happened lately to place the stock in its current price range.

I mainly check this only for stocks I am swing trading or day trading. If I were investing in this stock for a longer term, I would check several other aspects of the stock such as P/E ratios, news, dividend payouts, analysis, earnings, etc., but I will not get too specific about all those details in this book.

Tip Number Seven

Be wary of the perfect-looking chart set-up! I will admit that I put little faith in my personal ability to properly analyze the price movement of a stock based solely on looking at a chart pattern. So, perhaps I'm being a little too harsh on the chart aspect...

I do know of successful traders who choose swing trades simply based on chart movement. I do have some chart trading setups that I watch when I am swing trading and/or day trading a familiar stock, but I have learned NOT to **pick** a stock or make a BIG trading decision based solely on a pattern or a setup that I THINK I *might* see in a chart!

Why? Well, I have been so sure at times that I could see a perfect money-making opportunity based on a chart pattern, and I just knew it would go up in the next few trading days. So, I stepped outside the neutral zone, ignored my trading rules, and convinced myself to trade a stock that I did not know very well. To make matters worse, I would purchase far more shares than I should have because I was so *certain* about this good money-making opportunity. Then the next day or two comes around, and sadly, I've often discovered that I was wrong more times than I've ever been right.

Certainly, charts are good to watch over time, and they can show you points of resistance and support as well as many other valuable signals that can help you when you are trading familiar stocks. Still, my caution would be not to choose a stock in the spur of the moment, and then take a large position based on something you **think** you see in the chart—unless you have considerable experience reading charts and have developed a proven trading strategy.

Expert chart analysts are often very crafty when they give their chart analysis or predictions. You will hear them say something to the effect of "IF the stock does this and IF it does that, then it is POSSIBLE it will do THIS or do THAT." Well, okay, that analysis sounds pretty convincing to me, right?

So, once again, the moral to the story is this: NEVER choose a stock to trade in the spur of a moment and invest more money than you would have originally invested simply based on your confidence of a chart pattern or movement you feel will play out on the chart in the near future. Inevitably, the one time you do move too quickly and pick a stock to trade too soon, you might wander outside the neutral zone and go **all in** simply based on your confidence of the movement that the **chart** shows. Then the stock will do something radically different than what anyone thought or expected, and you will lose your socks. And sadly, I am speaking from experience.

I believe it's wise to study charts and learn all you can, but I feel that trying to become a chart reading expert should not be your number-one priority. Because of this fact, I will not be going into detail on the technical aspects for chart reading in this book either.

As I have already mentioned, I know many traders do make very good money choosing swing trades solely based on the chart patterns, and they have obviously developed very good trading systems to do so. However, I have not found it to be my strong point as a successful method for me; therefore, I must stick to what I know and teach in this book. I want to wrap up my tips in this chapter and put all this information I have shared to use.

A Recap

1. Make a list of all the companies you know and/or companies you use their products and/or services.
2. Put them on the priority list if their stocks are priced in the $10 or higher per share price range.
3. Check the stock's daily volume to see if the stock trades at least 500K shares or more per day on average. However, this tip is not essential if you really like a stock as there are some very good stocks with lower volume.
4. Choose stocks with a dividend, especially when looking for long-term growth stocks. Again, this is not a hard-and-set rule, but I tend to favor stocks with a dividend payout.
5. Check to see when the company will report earnings. I always like to study a stock through at least one earnings report to see how the company reacts and to get a current update on the health of the company. It also helps to monitor how the stock reacts to an earnings call and how it trades leading up into an earnings call.
6. Check the 52-week high and low to see where the stock is currently trading in regard to what the highest and lowest it has been.
7. Be wary of the perfect-looking chart set-up!

Once you have a nice group of stocks for potential swing trade candidates, then save them to a watchlist or what I like to call a "basket of goodie stocks." Before you ever make a swing trade, you will want to study and carefully monitor those stocks from several weeks to several months to learn all you can about each stock and their trading patterns and habits. **This step is vital to your success!**

When you watch stocks for a long enough period of time, you will begin to notice areas where they tend to pullback after hitting resistance, as well as areas of support where they tend to go up. You can also get updated analysis by experts as they give price target updates, commentary, and other news or reports on the company. I also believe to wait and see how a stock does leading up to and through at least one earnings report before you ever start swing trading that stock is VERY important.

As time goes on, you will build a nice little watchlist or basket of stocks that you are familiar with, and then you can monitor them for good swing trade opportunities.

> *"Rule number one: Don't lose money. Rule number two: Don't forget rule number one."*
>
> —Warren Buffett

> *"October: This is one of the peculiarly dangerous months to speculate in stocks. The others are July, January, September, April, November, May, March, June, December, August and February."*
>
> —Mark Twain

CHAPTER 4

The Positive Winning Mindset

Okay, now for the "meat and potatoes" of winning in this stock market game...

> *"It is impossible to produce superior performance unless you do something different from the majority."*
>
> —John Templeton

I have already periodically mentioned the importance of staying in the neutral zone, controlling your emotions and developing a positive winning mindset. I will continue to emphasize staying in the neutral zone by controlling your emotions and having a positive winning mindset all throughout this book. I greatly credit these two key factors to attributing to my successes in trading and investing in stocks.

I do feel that the catalyst behind a positive winning mindset, which has propelled me to a successful stock trading and investing career, was in developing a simple set of trading and investing rules which I will share in greater detail. These rules have helped me to develop and maintain a positive winning mindset and, by far, have been the most valuable asset for me to become a successful stock trader and investor.

So, what exactly is a positive winning mindset all about and how can you really develop it?

As I am writing this chapter, it is approaching midnight. I had actually closed down my laptop and settled into bed a few hours ago, but then a thought hit me like a lightning bolt and woke me up. I sat up straight in bed and knew that I had to record my thoughts immediately, or they might slip away before I woke in the morning.

I knew what a positive winning mindset meant to me personally as it has become a part of my trading DNA. However, I struggled with exactly how to put that mindset into clear-cut words so that my readers and coaching clients would have an explicit understanding of how to develop and rely on the same mindset for themselves. Then I realized that I simply need to share my set of trading rules and stress the importance of staying disciplined to follow them. Truly, following my trading rules and principles is really what gives me a positive winning mindset!

Tommy's 7 + 1 Stock Trading and
Investing Rules to Success:

1. Buy stock in companies you know and understand.
2. Always stay in the neutral zone.
3. Invest in yourself!
4. Scale into a stock slowly.
5. Always keep some cash on the sidelines.
6. Identify your price targets.
7. *Quick Charge Your Life!*

Bonus Rule: Laugh often!

To me, my having a positive winning mindset is accomplished by simply being disciplined to follow my trading rules. I know that if I follow my trading rules, I WILL have an edge to WINNING the stock trading game!

I will cover most of these trading rules in much more detail in the pages ahead. For this chapter, I want to briefly address each one of these rules to give you a basic understanding of what truly gives me a positive winning mindset. My goal is to help you develop the same type of mindset.

Rule Number 1: Buy stock in companies you know and understand.

> *"Behind every stock is a company. Find out what it's doing."*
>
> —Peter Lynch

When I have a positive winning mindset, I always remind myself to follow the stock tips that I outlined in chapter 3. I do not go chasing after the next best stock simply because I saw an ad online or because others are talking about a HOT new stock. I covered this rule in detail in chapter 3 by outlining the tips I use to choose good stocks to watch and trade.

If a stock makes sense to me, i.e., I can understand what makes it tick, and if I am familiar with the company and its products or services, then I do my due diligence as I already outlined to see if I want to add it to one of my trading watchlist baskets.

In the past, I would often get caught up in trying to chase after the next great stock to buy. So, I would jump around trading this stock and then that stock, but I never did all that well. However, I have since found that my time and money is much better spent just sticking with a small basket of stocks that I know and study in depth. I watch the company's overall performance and their trading patterns for a good period of time to build a winning relationship.

Rule Number 2: Always stay in the neutral zone.

> *"The individuals who cannot master their emotions are ill-suited to profit from the investment process."*
>
> —Benjamin Graham

When I have a positive winning mindset, I will remain in the neutral zone and not allow my emotions or mind to wander too far left into market fear or too far right into greed. I know I must stay in the neutral zone. The market will take you on a rollercoaster ride, so you must constantly be focused. Stay in the neutral zone and do not allow the ride to influence your trading decisions.

If I know my stock well, and the market has a few rough days in the red, possibly an opportunity is being presented to me to purchase more stock while it is on sale. On the opposite side, when there are some strong green days and my stock has reached its price target or I am up a good percentage in a growth stock, then I must be disciplined to trim my position and take a profit rather than becoming greedy by trying to get more out of the trade than perhaps what the market or stock is willing to give.

Rule Number 3: Invest in yourself.

> *"Spend each day trying to be a little wiser than you were when you woke up."*
>
> —Charlie Munger

When I have a positive winning mindset, I continually look for ways to improve myself by watching inspirational videos and reading books about success and investing. I want to glean whatever knowledge I can use that might strengthen my trading rules and give me an even greater edge.

I also enjoy attending church and engaging in hobbies apart from stock trading such as golfing, fishing, watching sports on TV or attending local college sporting events with friends and family. All of these various activities bring me great joy and satisfaction.

When I developed the *Quick Charge Concept* program, I created a formula for my coaching clients called the "Secret Sauce Formula" to success. (I will share a little more about this success formula in a later chapter.) I learned that if you will adhere to the practice of continually investing into yourself daily, your chances of success in stock trading and in life as well will greatly increase.

Rule Number 4: Scale into a stock slowly.

> *"The easiest way to manage your money is to take it one step at a time and not worry about being perfect."*
>
> —Ramit Sethi

When I have a positive winning mindset, I must discipline myself to enter a position with a smaller portion of my initial investment. I usually initiate a trade with about half of my intended investment. By doing this, if the stock pulls back some, I am allowing myself the opportunity to possibly purchase more shares at a lower price. However, if the stock does not pull back, I will still be set up to make a nice profit on the run up.

I also know that by following this particular rule, I will not lose as much money. For example, if the stock suddenly drops down and stops me out after my initial smaller purchase, then I will not lose as much money. Not losing a great deal of money, in turn, helps me to better manage my emotions. I have also found that if the pullback or drop in price does not stop me out and finds support above my stop level, then I can add more shares and dollar average down to make even more profit as well.

To help me stay focused, I have a saying firmly implanted into my mind that helps to remind me of the very important rule number 4:

Never buy in amounts that make you nervous.

I know that I should never go **all in** or use up more of my portfolio funds on a trade than what I feel comfortable. If you feel the constant need or urge to watch a stock trade out of fear, you might have invested way more money into that trade than what you should have. That fear, my friend, is a fairly good indication that you have already invested way **too much** money into that trade, and you have lost your winning edge.

Rule Number 5: Always keep some cash on the sidelines.

> *"We don't have to be smarter than the rest, we have to be more disciplined than the rest."*
>
> —Warren Buffett

When I have a positive winning mindset, I am disciplined to always keep some cash on the sidelines at all times. When I have cash on the sidelines, I am always ready for good buying opportunities. The market will often offer some golden buying opportunities, so the investor must always have some cash in reserve to take full advantage of those big price drop opportunities.

Rule Number 6: Identify your price targets.

> *"One of the funny things about the stock market is that every time one person buys, another sells, and both think they are astute."*
>
> —William Feather

When I have a positive winning mindset, I determine three key price targets or price points before I ever enter a swing trade.

Point One is my stop loss point. How much money am I willing to possibly lose? Your stop limit is usually set right below where support can be found on a chart. If the stock falls below this support level, then it is best to be stopped out of the stock.

Point Two is my entry point. Figuring out at what price point you feel comfortable entering the stock is so important.

Point Three is your price target or PT for where you will sell or trim your stock for some profit.

Rule Number 7: *Quick Charge Your Life!*

When I have a positive winning mindset, I remember to always *Quick Charge My Life!*

The *quick-charge* life is about developing a personal relationship with the Lord and continually seeking Him to energize you with His power. It's about taking responsibility for your happiness by thinking positive thoughts—no matter what you may encounter in life. *Quick charging* is about learning to be calm and trusting the Lord during the storms in your life. It's about finding joy and blessing when you inspire others. It's also about generously giving of all that God has given you. In a nutshell, the *Quick Charge Life* is an invitation for you to intentionally, deliberately and consciously change the way you think so that you might discover all the *quick-charge* outlets with which God surrounds you every single day of your life. The *quick-charge* concept will allow you to continually charge the power already living within you to move past your perceived limitations and boldly step into the life you were born to create. Learn it, live it, and inspire others...*Quick Charge Your Life!*

Bonus Rule: Laugh often!

> *"Always laugh when you can, it is cheap medicine."*
>
> —Lord Byron

When I have a positive winning mindset, I remember to laugh often. Just make yourself laugh as often as possible every day. Perhaps you can watch something funny online or on TV or read a funny joke. Do whatever it takes to help make yourself laugh. Laughing is good medicine for the soul. Laughter will help give you better focus when you're trading. Laughter releases built-up tensions and will help you stay in the neutral zone and on top of your game. Laughing often and seeing the humor in life truly is one of the key secrets to success.

> *"In many ways, the stock market is like the weather in that if you don't like the current conditions all you have to do is wait a while."*
>
> —Low Simpson

CHAPTER 5

How Much to Get Started?

I contemplated removing this chapter from the book, as having ample funds to invest would be so convenient. However, I know that "How much?" is a pressing question that many have. I guess this question should be addressed before getting too deep into the book. However, I do not know if there really is a concise, straightforward answer or a simplified formula to use to answer this question.

When I first started trading my own stocks online in 1998, I made an initial deposit of $2,500 to open my online brokerage account with Scottrade, but again, I don't know if there really is a correct amount to get started. At the time, I believe that $2,500 was the minimum amount an investor could deposit to open an account, so that is the amount I started with.

After that initial deposit, I added to my account little by little when I could, and my account balance went up and down for a few years, never really growing considerably. I did not possess the knowledge and trading skills that I needed in order to help me start winning in the stock market game back then.

I often have one question I like to ask people when I am asked, "How much money do I need to get started?"

Question:
"How much money can you afford to lose?"

Investing in the stock market can be very risky at times, and if you jump in with both feet believing that you're going to be rich soon, then you are *not* thinking clearly. As I have already made mention, my stock trading account went up and down for several years as I formulated my trading rules and discovered my positive winning mindset. As time went on, I was finally able to deposit more money into my account so I could invest more, but I was also armed with my trading rules and a new positive winning mindset to finally win at the stock trading game.

What it really comes down to is your risk tolerance and goals. Many investors want to throw a couple hundred dollars into a penny stock and hope it skyrockets quickly so they can make a fortune. Yes, I suppose that dream is always possible, but chances are much greater that you'll crash and burn and lose a good portion of your investment funds—if not all.

I do realize that $2,500 might be a sizable amount for many to get started. I would say that you do need at least $1,000 in order to get a fair start in the online trading/investing world. If you can afford to fund your account with more than that, then you'll have even more opportunity to grow your account more quickly.

So, let me help you put together a quick trading plan if you are starting with a minimum investment of at least $1,000. I will assume that you already know how to open a brokerage account online in order to buy and sell stocks. If not, then search online for brokerage firms and study what you find. You will find plenty of advice to help you get started.

Once you have opened an account and deposited some money, you are now ready to get started!

First, follow the tips I shared in chapter 3 for finding good stocks to put into your watch basket. Before you start doing any stock trading, I suggest you keep a close eye on that list of stocks you have put into a watchlist basket. Of vital importance is conducting diligent research on these stocks and watching them for several weeks to several months before ever trying to make a trade.

However, as you are watching your basket of stocks for potential swing trade candidates, you can get started with an initial dividend stock investment. I would suggest finding a solid dividend stock and only buy 3 to 5 shares just to get your feet wet. Then let that stock continue to pay you dividends over time.

You can buy a decent dividend stock for around $10 to $15 per share. So, for this example, if you're starting out with an account balance of one thousand dollars, I would suggest buying perhaps 5 shares of a $15 per share dividend stock. 5 shares x $15 = $75 invested.

Now, you have officially started your investing career, and you still have a good portion of your funds ($925) to work with for swing trading. But you now have a stock in your portfolio that will hopefully be paying you dividends for as long as you own it. If the stock drops in price, you can add a couple more shares and continue to build on your position over time.

Possibly the stock you buy as a long-term dividend investment stock may also be a good swing trade candidate as well. I have several stocks that I hold in my long-term basket in one account and then use the same stock for swing trade opportunities in another account. (I'll cover dividend investing in more detail in a later chapter.)

Next, I would suggest you buy a few shares in a stock you feel has good long-term growth potential. This should be a stock that you are familiar with and has a good business model and proven success. You should check out the analyst reports, P/E (Price to Earnings), past earnings reports, recent news, and also see what analysts are projecting for future growth for the stock. I would suggest looking for stocks in the $25 to $50 per share range to start. Once you find one you like, then purchase 2 to 5 shares and tuck them away. 2 shares x $35 = $70 invested.

Continue to monitor those stocks and research them each week to see what they are doing to stay successful. I remember Jim Cramer once saying on his television show *Mad Money* that for any stock you hold in your portfolio, you should be willing to conduct at least one hour of research per week.

Next, I would do some quick research to find a few penny stocks being actively traded and check the history of those stocks. Once you find some stocks, and after researching, you like their story, product or service and potential for possible future growth that trade in 25¢ to $1 range, then go ahead and purchase 50 shares of a couple different penny stocks and set them aside. Maybe you'll get lucky and hit a winner but understand that you may be throwing away your money as well. I do believe they are worth the gamble—in case you do find a good one.

I rarely ever buy a stock in the penny or low-dollar range these days, but I have purchased many stocks in the past in the 25¢ to $1.00 price range in hopes of getting lucky prior to developing my trading rules and positive winning mindset. Truthfully, I have probably lost more money than I have gained on these types of investments, but if you must, I do understand the hope for something really good to happen, and certainly, it is always possible.

So, let's say you've done your due diligence and researched several penny stocks and found a couple that look good to you. So, you buy 50 shares of XYZ penny stock at 40¢ per share for a total cost of $20.

Next you buy 50 shares of ZYX penny stock at 50¢ per share = a total cost of $25.

Now you've given yourself an opportunity to maybe hit a good stock and make some money to add to your portfolio. However, it's also possible you're going to lose the money you've invested.

Let's recap and do the math.

You started with $1,000 and purchased 5 shares of a good dividend stock for $15 per share = -$75, leaving you with a balance of $925.

Next you purchased 2 shares of a solid growth stock for $35 per share = - $70, leaving you with a balance of $855.

Next, you purchased 50 shares of XYZ penny stock @ 40¢ per share = - $20, leaving you with a balance of $835.

Next you purchased 50 shares of ZYX penny stock @ 50¢ per share = - $25, leaving you with a balance of $810 for swing trading. I do not suggest trying to day trade until your account balance grows much larger, and you are much more familiar with trading stocks in general.

The time has now come to get creative and build up your cash. Anytime you can add more money to your account, then I would encourage you to discipline yourself to continue adding more cash to the account.

Whenever a stock in your dividend or long-term growth portfolio has a pullback, you should consider buying another share or two as well to keep building on your positions.

So, what do you do with $810?

I already discussed in an earlier chapter that I suggest you start slowly and buy in smaller lots as you learn to trade. I will continue to delve deeper into my trading and investing strategies in the pages ahead, but my favorite method of trading is **swing trading** stocks. Basically, when you swing trade, you are holding the shares for a few days to a few weeks while looking for a move in price to make a profit.

So, you'll want to research to find some good stocks that you know something about the company and/or products and then watch them for a while to learn their tendencies as outlined in chapter 3. DO NOT dive right in and start swing trading the stocks you place in your watch list. Always research and watch them for a while as you add more money to your account, and when you're ready to start trading, I always suggest buying a small position and scale in slowly as you learn.

What I see most beginners tend to do is take $500 and purchase 100 shares of a $5 stock, hoping it goes up to $6 or more per share over a period of a few weeks. That's a $1+ increase in stock price, and they would make a profit of about $100.

Yes, certainly this can happen, but I really feel it is far better to find a higher priced stock to swing trade. The higher the price of the stock, the better chance of greater price movement. That does not mean there are not plenty of good stocks in the $5 price range that won't move a significant amount in a short period of time, but a $5 stock requires much more momentum to move to $6 versus a $20 stock to move to $21 or a $100 stock to move to $101.

So, if you only have roughly $800 to work with, then I suggest you purchase 8 to 15 shares of a higher priced stock. You might make a smaller profit over buying more shares of a lower cost stock if the lower priced stock were to go up nicely, but, more than likely, the higher priced stock will reach your price targets much faster.

Suppose you have been watching a stock in your swing trade basket that is currently trading around $20 per share. You do not want to take more than half of your initial position just in case it drops substantially in price and stops you out or pulls back to give you the opportunity to buy more at a slightly lower price. So, risk no more than about $200 to $300 to initiate the position, which would get you about 10 to 15 shares.

So, let's say you buy 10 shares of the $20 stock, and over the next three weeks, it goes up 7.5% to $21.50, and you sell it. You would have made a $15 profit! ($1.50 per share x 10 shares = $15).

As I said, the chances that a higher priced stock will have more price movement allows you to make quicker profits as you learn with a smaller account. So, once you close the trade, you can then move on to another swing trade.

Again, unless one of your penny stocks skyrockets or you were fortunate enough to swing trade a $5 dollar stock that jumped to $10, then, in my opinion, you are better off to play higher priced stocks that have a much better chance of moving much more, and making $10, $20, $30 or more in profit per swing trade. As mentioned earlier, I do not suggest you try to start off day trading until you have much more money in your account and a good understanding of the trading world.

Day trading is a whole other animal. Ultimately, one of the best ways to invest is to buy good stocks and hold them for a long period of time. Then trim them a bit as they rise and buy more shares when they dip, but where's the fun in that, right? You might be surprised... That is fun too, but let's keep learning.

> *"Before you speak, listen. Before you write, think. Before you spend, earn. Before you invest, investigate. Before you criticize, wait. Before you pray, forgive. Before you quit, try. Before you retire, save. Before you die, give."*
>
> —William A. Ward

CHAPTER 6

Set Reasonable Goals

One mistake I often see most beginning traders make is setting their goals way too high. Why do they set their goals so high? Well, unfortunately, I feel most people who show some interest in learning how to trade stocks online are influenced by ads claiming you can make $500 to $1,000 per day trading stocks or make $5K to $10K per month swing trading or day trading.

Yes, it is very possible to make this kind of money and even much more in due time, but you should start slowly while you build up your account and develop your trading skills, or you will run the risk of quickly going broke.

When I'm speaking of setting reasonable goals, I am mainly talking about setting goals for swing trading and not day trading or long-term investing. I do not recommend even trying to day trade until you are extremely familiar with the trading landscape in general and have successfully been swing trading for a while.

Okay, so when you are just getting started with swing trading, you should set reasonable goals of $10 to $40 profit per swing trade while you learn and build a relationship with your stocks. Now, when your goal is to make $10 to $40 on a swing trade, then your loss tolerance or allowance should only be about $10 to $40 loss as well…

Pay close attention to this next point…do NOT take on too large of a position when you initiate a swing trade. I know, I know…I have already said this a few times before, but it is a key component of my trading rules. Buying larger amounts of stock trying to make more money can be so tempting. However, you need to scale into a trade gradually. I cannot emphasize enough how this is such an important aspect of developing a positive winning mindset.

I know you want to make tons of money, and I know making a ton of money when you are buying smaller amounts of stock and making smaller profits is harder. However, the methods I use to teach others to make money through investing and trading stocks starts out by learning the skills and disciplines to make money in smaller amounts as you develop your skills.

This rule also protects you from losing a ton of money and quickly wiping out your account like 90 percent of the beginning traders who end up doing exactly that. Sadly, they never become successful stock traders!

So, learn to master the $10 profit level, then $20 profit levels and so on by taking on smaller positions. Once you can consistently do well making small swing trades and getting $10 to $40 profit out of the trade, then you can aim for $50 to $100 per swing trade in profit and so on…

You will increase your profits by simply making the same trade as before but taking on a slightly larger position. However, trying to scale up too quickly will likely end up costing you money. So, please take my suggestions here and master each level—$10, $20, $40, $50, then $100 per swing trade and so on… Just continue to scale up your position size slowly in order to achieve these goals. This will help you build your trading skills and mindset into a winning trader.

So, let's look at an example of another swing trade using a small trade size. In chapter 5 we addressed the question of how much money do you need to get started. In that chapter I suggested that you start with at least $1000 to get started, but if you recall we only had $810 to work with after some initial investments in a growth stock and dividend stock. So, I will be using that $810 account balance as my starting point.

In this next example swing trade, we will take a position in an even higher priced stock... With this trade I will also introduce the stop limit and price target profit percentage rules.

We will be using a 7% stop limit and 7.5% profit price target.

So, let's say you have a stock XYZ in your trading basket that you've been watching for some time, and you see a potentially good opportunity to swing trade this stock.

XYZ is currently trading at $79.50 per share.

One of the analysts covering this stock has recently put out a new price target of $98 per share. Now, there is no time frame for when this stock will hit that $98 price point, but that is the price target the stock is projected to reach in a reasonable period of time.

So, the goal is $20 to $40+ profit on this trade.

Let's say you hope to buy a total of 8 shares, but you will only purchase 1/2 of your initial position, so you would purchase 4 shares to initiate the trade.

However, before you ever enter the trade, you already know you do not want to lose more than about $20 to $40 or so on this trade if it does not work out. This number is based on the number of shares you will be purchasing and the amount of price drop you will allow for the stop loss point before the stocks would be sold off at a loss should the trade not work out.

So, you will first calculate a stop limit price point based on the projected entry price that you'll enter the trade.

Now, let's assume that you're planning to enter the stock at $80.25 per share and purchase 4 shares.

4 shares X $80.25 per share = $321 invested

Once you purchase 4 shares at $80.25 then you will set a stop limit order 7% below the purchase price.

$80.25 – 7% = $74.63 or $5.62 in loss

So, your stop limit point will be set at $74.63.

However, before you initiate a trade, you want to check the support level on the chart to see if $74.63 is below that level (Support level materializes when a stock price drops to a level that prompts traders to buy.) If the stop point is below support, that is good. If the stock drops in price, then chances are buyers will start coming back into the stock prior to it hitting your stop loss point! However, if the stock drops down below the support level after your initial purchase of 4 shares and stops you out, then you stand to lose $22.48 on this trade with only 4 shares.

Next, you calculate what a 7.5% gain would be to see how that correlates with the price target set by the analyst.

$80.25 + 7.5% = $86.27

This is well below the projected price target of $98 per share set by the analyst, so this seems to be a good swing trade as you do not want to be too aggressive.

At this point you're ready to initiate 1/2 of your intended position with a "limit" buy order of 4 shares at a limit price of $80.25 per share. When you place a limit order, you are saying you do not want to purchase for any higher price than the price you set—$80.25 per share. After you purchase the shares, then you will want to immediately set your stop limit order at $74.63, which will be 7% below the $80.25 where you purchased. It is also important to be certain that you set this order as GTC (Good Till Cancelled) as this ensures that your order stays in the system and does not expire until executed or canceled.

If you do not understand what a stop limit to sell or limit order to buy is or any other terms mentioned, then I suggest searching online or look in the help section at your online broker for assistance in learning these terms and how to properly place these orders. Understanding the differences between limit orders and market orders and the risk involved with each is extremely important.

After you make your purchase of 4 shares and set your stop limit, you will watch the stock and see if you get a pullback in the price below your initial purchase price. If the stock pulls back on light volume, then you can choose to add 4 more shares. If it does not pull back, then you'll just ride the initial position up to your $86.27 or more price target if a buying opportunity does not arise.

Now let's look at the numbers! If the stock does not pull back allowing you to add 4 more shares, then you will ride your initial 4 shares up to the price target of $86.27 or greater...

Based on your purchase price of $80.25 per share, then you have a gain of roughly $6 per share.

$6 X 4 shares = $24 profit

If, however, you do get a slight pullback and add 4 more shares, then you stand to make even more.

Let's say a few days after you purchased the initial 4 shares at $80.25, the stock pulls back to $78.55 per share, and there are no bad reports on the stock. Perhaps the stock is simply dropping back some on market news not directly related to your stock. If it does pull back, then I like to look at the volume during the pull back to make sure it's not a sell off. If the volume is light or normal, then there is no reason to believe that it's not a good trade, so I would want to add to my position to dollar average down.

For this example, let's suppose that, from all indications, the stock is still healthy so you take advantage of this buying opportunity and add 4 more shares at $78.55 per share. This purchase now gives you an average purchase price of $79.40 per share for your 8 shares.

After you purchase the additional 4 shares, be sure to edit your stop limit order number of shares to sell 8 shares, but DO NOT adjust your stop loss down as you will still leave it set at $74.63.

If the swing trade works out to be a win and goes up to your price target of $86.27 or more, then you have a better profit. $79.40 average purchase price per share x 8 shares @ $6.87 per share profit = $54.96 total profit!

Certainly, $54.96 may not seem like a fortune, but the disciplines and lessons you will learn as you continue to execute smaller swing trades with much less risk will lead to making much more profit down the road. Far too many inexperienced traders will blow up their accounts after three or four swing trades trying to chase every new stock idea and play with $1, $2, $5 stocks and penny stocks, buying far too many shares.

Think about this: if you were to consistently average $100 to $300 per month in profit for the next 12 months using the swing trade method I have described in this chapter, then you will have accumulated another $1,200 to $3,600 in your account to work with in only 1 year. If you originally started with only $1,000, then you would have more than doubled your account size in 12 months! If you do that every year for a few years, then you will build a decent amount of cash to trade with. As your cash balance grows, you can gradually increase your share sizes for greater profits. Do understand, though, you are taking on more risk with greater losses as well.

If you're dreaming of making enough money to buy a Lamborghini or a Ferrari and private jets, then you are missing the point! Yes, it is possible to make really good money in the stock market, but doing so requires many hours of watching stocks in your baskets, following a disciplined set of rules, keeping a positive winning mindset, building up a large amount of cash to work with, and continuously working on improving yourself, as well as a bit of good fortune.

The following are some fundamental truths and principles I discovered that are well worth keeping in front of you at all times to remind yourself of the game you are playing.

Five Fundamental Truths of Trading Stocks

1. **Anything** can happen.
2. You don't need to know what is going to happen next to make money.
3. There is a random distribution between wins and losses for any given set of variables that define an edge.
4. An edge is nothing more than an indication of a higher probability of one thing happening over another.
5. Every moment in the market is unique.

Seven Principles of Consistency

1. You objectively identify your edges.
2. You predefine the risk of every trade.
3. You completely accept the risk, or you are willing to let go of the trade.
4. You act on your edges without reservation or hesitation.
5. You pay yourself as the market makes money available to you.
6. You continually monitor your susceptibility for making errors.
7. You understand the absolute necessity of these principles of consistent success and, therefore, you never violate them.

I cannot emphasize enough the importance of starting with reasonable goals and initiating smaller positions. Slowly scale up to stay within your neutral zone. Most people will set too high of a goal to get started, chase everything under the sun, then spend far too much money purchasing services and/or products while trying to reach those high goals. They generally fall into the 90 percent of traders who fail to win at this game. When you finally learn that you do not need a degree in stock trading and you do not need to understand all that is going on in order to make a very nice return, then you can begin the journey of success.

> *"The person who doesn't know where his next dollar is coming from usually doesn't know where his last dollar went."*
>
> —Author Unknown

> *"When you understand that your self-worth is not determined by your net-worth, then you'll have financial freedom."*
>
> —Suze Orman

CHAPTER 7

You Are a Goldfish

A wealthy investor once said, "When you are trading in the stock market, you are competing against ME *[the wealthy investor]...* and all the other extremely wealthy sharks in the trading world as well. So, you better be on your game!"

The fact is the big shark traders have multi-millions and even billions of dollars with which to play this game. They have sophisticated services and tools that the average trader simply does not have the financial means to afford or gain access to. These investors have access to teams of intelligent and seasoned people who spend hours upon hours researching, evaluating, and calculating each stock for the best trade potential.

I am certain I did not get this statement exactly word for word, but I do believe I captured the essence of their thoughts and the general idea of what this big investing shark was saying.

Whenever I am trading in the market, I often recall this statement because I must always remember many wealthy sharks are playing the same stock trading game that I am playing, but they are playing with much deeper pockets. They also possess far more sophisticated tools than I have. The reality is that the retail investor is only a tiny "goldfish" swimming amongst the big and powerful sharks...

As I have already mentioned in the introduction, I have no clue what the title, subtitle or other design aspects for this book will be. I happened to see an image very fitting for this chapter that was created during the brainstorming design process for another book I wrote in my *Quick Charge* series. When I was working on my cover for the book titled *Quick Charge Your Life - Unshakable Self-Esteem,* my designer sent a few cover concepts for me to consider as possibilities. I liked one concept in particular that portrayed a goldfish swimming with a shark. That cover did not make the cut for that book, but I felt the concept was a powerful and fitting image for this particular chapter.

A shark fin was strapped to the goldfish's back as it boldly swam alongside a furious-looking shark. The cover was portraying the goldfish's basically saying, "I may look like a goldfish, but inside I feel like I am a shark too. I'm not afraid of the big bad shark!" One day I will likely use that cover for one of my *Quick Charge* series books, but that idea is so apropos for this particular chapter.

To me, the goldfish represents a retail trader like you and me. However, when you develop a positive winning mindset, you can put on a shark fin and swim with confidence amongst the sharks. The big sharks are swimming all around you, devouring large chunks of shares and making millions and even billions of dollars every year, but there is still plenty of money for the confident and wise goldfish to devour.

Just because we goldfish are swimming with the sharks that does not mean we will become their lunch. There is still plenty of room for the confident goldfish to swim in the same waters as the shark and make a nice profit year after year playing the game.

Let me share a secret: the wealthy investors must have an even sharper positive winning mindset; otherwise, they will not be able to maintain their wealthy shark status. In fact, another shark is likely to come along and take a big bite out of them if they lose their edge.

The retail trader is only a small goldfish compared to all of the big sharks swimming in the trading investing world. However, those sharks do not want to waste their time trying to chase and eat the wise and disciplined goldfish. So, don your shark fin and swim with confidence. You can also win at this game!

I want to call your attention to a particular **word** that I have used frequently in these first few chapters. I feel pointing out that noun is important to help you understand how it fits in the trading world. That word is GAME. Yes, the stock market is a GAME with winners and losers every day. You are competing against millions of other traders when you make a trade. One trader feels he is right when he sells; the other trader feels he is right when he buys.

Some traders, who are called the bears, are convinced the stock will go down. Other traders, who are called the bulls, are playing the stock to go up. The stock is available under the same set of factors, but one trader (the bear) can see a down trend while another trader (the bull) is betting it will go on an uptrend.

I love watching sports, and I am especially fond of college sports. I really love watching college football and women's college basketball and softball. I am fortunate to live in a state that currently has some of the best woman's college basketball teams in America—the Oregon Ducks and Oregon State Beavers. I greatly appreciate the game and enjoy watching many other teams around the country play as well.

A few key elements in many sports are closely related to stock trading. So, when I am trading, I am often looking at the whole process of buying and selling stocks as an important **game**.

In most team sports, each athlete has his specialty or position. In football some of the athletes are good at catching the ball, so they become receivers. Some athletes have quick feet, so they often become running backs or play other positions where their speed will benefit the team. The big guys play on the line, and those who are good at seeing the whole field and throwing the ball often become quarterbacks.

In the stock trading game, some of the "players" include day traders, swing traders, and growth stock investors. The big hedge fund managers handle large accounts. Some traders only buy options, and others only buy the stock itself. Some players focus on dividend stocks, and others trade futures or forex and so on...

Another aspect of the sports game is that some players are better suited for offense while others are best on defense. Once an athlete reaches a professional level in football, he is often a specialist in one position, which helps determine if that position is offensive or defensive.

Football and basketball coaches often say that the defense wins games while others might argue that if a team is not scoring points on offense then that team cannot win the game, and so on.

"What does any of this have to do with stock trading?" you ask.

I'm glad you asked because offense and defense have much to do with the stock trading game. When it comes to stock trading, I believe that a good **defense** is actually more important than a good offense. I might even argue that playing good defense is better than a good offense in sports in that the fewer points the opponents scores, the better the chances for the home team to overtake them. However, that's a debate for a different time. I do think you will soon see where I am headed with this point.

As I have already stated, the stock market is a game with traders who are on the side of the bulls, and they want to drive up the price of the stock. The traders who are on the side of the bears want to drive down the price of the stock. These traders are battling daily, and whether or not you realize it, you are part of this game and battle as well.

If you are "long a stock," which basically means you are betting that the stock will go up, then you are on the side of the bulls. If you are "short the stock," which means you borrowed money in a margin account to first sell a stock, then when the price goes down, you will purchase it back at a lower price. You are siding with the bears.

I don't want you to be confused at this point. Being a bull or a bear is not defense versus offense; it is simply the side or team you are choosing to play on for the stock game at any given time. The choice of bull or bear is based on the price action you feel will happen. Many stock traders will become a bear and play one stock short and then become a bull and play another stock long. This is simply the team or side they're choosing to play on during any particular part of the game and not offense versus defense.

So, what do I mean by playing defense versus offense when it comes to stock trading?

In this **game**, I want to zero in on playing good **defense** when it comes to stock trading. Defense is when you are protecting your losses, and offense is taking your profits. Both are important factors to consider when playing the game well, but I personally feel it is far better as a stock trader to be good at playing **defense** by limiting your losses than it is to be the best offensive player in making profits. If you learn to manage your losses well, then you have a much better chance at winning the game and making a steady profit when it comes to buying and selling stocks!

Whether your stock is going up or going down, you should always be paying more attention to your **defense**! If you're in a swing trade playing on the side of the bulls, but the stock is going down in favor of the bears, then you must be disciplined to set a stop limit. Do not allow yourself to be influenced into adjusting it down even further in order not to be stopped out because you think it might recover. Remember, always try to stay in the neutral zone. You are far better off to be stopped out and limit your losses. Thus, by limiting your losses and staying disciplined, you're playing smart defense.

If the stock has been going up, then you must be disciplined to trim your position or close out the trade for a profit and not be too greedy. This is considered good offense. Otherwise, if it pulls back, you will give away points by losing money. However, it always seems to be easier to play the game when you are making money on offense, so I feel defense takes far more discipline and is more important.

The other aspect of the game that I want to draw to your attention is knowing what position you play best. I am a swing trader. I have my trading rules, my swing trading plan, and I make most of my money by being the best swing trader I can be. Thus, I do not tinker with options or try to day trade much. I do not mess with trading futures or forex or any other types of trading strategies that would likely sidetrack me and cost me money.

The point is, don't spread yourself too thin trying to play options, day trade, swing trade, forex, futures, and on and on... Investigate the various types of investments or strategies, and maybe try a few to see what you like. Focus on becoming the best trader in whatever position you are best at. Perhaps you might like trading Forex or Futures. Maybe you would enjoy being an options trader or only a long-term dividend investor. My main position of focus is swing trader, but I also dabble in some long-term investing and dividend investing. My identity and specialty, though, is in swing trading.

Once you see the entire stock trading process as a game, you can figure out which position or style of trading you like best. Regardless of what position you decide to play, you need to become mindful of the process and think about your offensive and defensive moves. Always having a game plan and learning to execute your game plan well is vitally important.

> *"All sharks were born swimming."*
>
> —Rebecca McNutt

> *"The number-one job of the hedge-fund manager is not to make sure that you can retire with a smile on your face—it's for him to retire with a smile on his face."*
>
> —Mark Cuban

CHAPTER 8

The BIG Wins and the Momentary Blunder

> *"All you need for a lifetime of successful investing is a few big winners, and the pluses from those will overwhelm the minuses from the stocks that don't work out."*
>
> —Peter Lynch

In the past I have often dreamt of becoming a trading shark a time or two, but the more I live my life, I have come to realize that I do not want the additional pressures and responsibilities that come when dealing with hundreds of millions or billions of dollars.

I am a goldfish, and I will likely always be a goldfish. I am not just any goldfish though; I am a confident, successful, and happy swing trading goldfish! Being looked on as a goldfish swimming in a sea of sharks is perfectly fine with me.

I have learned to enjoy swimming with the big sharks! As I have learned to navigate my way through the shark-infested waters of the stock market, I have had some very BIG wins and a momentary blunder along the way as well.

Before I share the details on some of my BIG wins and my momentary blunder, I want to explain the reasoning for this chapter. I have included this chapter to prove that the little guy can also win. I am living proof that if you play the game well and stay disciplined to follow a solid set of rules, good things will come.

I can attest to the fact that the quote by Peter Lynch at the beginning of this chapter is true: *"All you need for a lifetime of successful investing is a few big winners, and the pluses from those will overwhelm the minuses from the stocks that don't work out."*

Yes, I am fortunate enough to be one of those who stayed with the game long enough to find some big winners. I want to encourage anyone reading this book who is still dreaming of hitting it BIG, that dreams really do come true!

Some of My BIG Wins

After several years of fine-tuning my trading rules and developing my positive winning mindset, I slowly learned the ropes of the trading and investing game. I was doing quite well by focusing on certain stocks and swing trading them. As I continued to add stocks to my trading basket, I began researching biotech stocks that were receiving some good press.

I came across one biotech company in particular that caught my attention called Novavax (NVAX). Based on my research on this biotech stock at the time, I felt purchasing some stock was a good, calculated risk with a potential reward, and I was willing to lose a few thousand in order to potentially make a few thousand.

I had executed many trades similar to this one in years past, and I had won on a few and lost on a few. However, during the time I was looking into this stock, the reviews certainly seemed to indicate a better risk/reward than many others in which I had invested in the past.

When I first initiated a position in (NVAX), I was very confident in the level of discomfort that I was willing to accept should the trade go bad, and I felt the potential upside was well worth the risk. So, I initiated a position in this stock when it was trading around $14 per share, and it quickly went up to $16 per share, so I sold it. Then it pulled back some, and I initiated another position around $14 per share again. This time it pulled back more, so I added more shares to average down on my overall price. As it continued to go up and down some in this range for a couple of weeks, I continued to add more shares. After I had accumulated a sizable position, I had an average price of just under $12 per share.

Just as I had anticipated, some really good news broke shortly after I had added to my position. However, the price jump far exceeded my expectations as the stock quickly soared or "gapped up" as they say in the trading world into the mid-$20 price range. So, I sold some of my position around $23 per share, and then it went up even more, so I sold the rest of my position around $27 per share as I anticipated a pull back.

Then the stock did exactly as I had anticipated and pulled back to around $18 per share. I initiated a new position, and it went up and down some as I again added more and more shares. Then as I had hoped, it gapped up again, but this time it went up substantially higher than the last time on even better news into the mid $40+ price range, giving me another HUGE win.

I took some more of my winnings, and based on all the research I had already done, I felt there was still more opportunity for this stock to go even higher, so I continued to invest a portion of my winnings back into (NVAX) as it steadily went up.

I was able to swing trade and day trade (NVAX) over and over for a period of about three months as it continued up for more additional profits as more and more news continued to break for this company in the Biotech sector. After a few consecutive months of winning trades and watching (NVAX) trade up into the $170 to $180 per share range, it began to cool down, so I started trading other stocks that I had been watching in my basket.

My next BIG win came when trading one of my all-time favorite stocks, Dollar General (DG). I had been watching and swing trading this stock for some time and made some very nice returns. After my big wins with Novavax (NVAX) I had substantially more capital to invest. As I gained confidence in trading Dollar General (DG), I began taking larger and larger positions. Then on one particular swing trade after I had accumulated a rather large position, it ran up nicely, and the payoff was sizable as well!

Wow! I was on a roll, baby! I felt invincible and started to dream of how I was going to dominate the trading world... My winning trade(s) in (NVAX) and (DG) as well as a couple others catapulted me into a whole new world of trading and investing. Within a matter of a few months, I had not only made up for all of my bad years, but I had literally stepped into a whole new level of trading ability.

At the time you are reading this chapter, there is no telling where (NVAX) will be trading at. It could be trading in the $200, $300, $500 ++ price range or it could be trading at $1 to $3 per share or even gone. The same is true for (DG), but I feel Dollar General will have great success and be a good stock for trading, as well as one for holding as a long-term investment as well.

Now as I mentioned, because of this series of big wins I had substantially more money to work with, and I discovered a whole new world of trading in the stock market game. I guess you could say I was a slightly bigger goldfish, though still a goldfish nonetheless.

Each month I was able to take on more trades and more risk while increasing my share size... However, I quickly lost my edge, and for lack of a better explanation, I got way too BIG for my britches. Unfortunately, I learned very quickly that getting overconfident is one of the worst places to be as a stock trader—when you are a goldfish swimming with sharks.

Although it hurts to admit it now, I had a momentary blunder, which came while trading Netflix (NFLX). However, that loss was the biggest wakeup call and blessing I could've asked for. *What?*

"How in the world can losing a good chunk of money ever be a blessing?" you might ask.

Well, that blunder gave me a *quick charge* and reminded me that I needed to stay humble and stick to my trading rules and positive winning mindset that I know and teach.

I was very familiar with Netflix as well as their services, and I also understood why Netflix was surging up. After all, familiarizing myself with a particular stock is part of my trading rules and practices for choosing stocks to trade, or I would've avoided the trade all together.

However, I BROKE one of my **key** trading rules by putting way too much money in to start with when initiating my initial position. Why did I do this? Well, Netflix (NFLX) had been running up and up for weeks, and I felt like it was going to the moon. I *thought* I could not possibly lose. Unfortunately, I jumped into (NFLX) with both feet.

The fact is when you **break** a trading rule, it is likely going to **break** you!

When I entered my big winning trade(s), I knew what my loss tolerance was and what my potential gains could possibly be as well, but I generally initiated smaller positions to start and then built my positions into larger holdings as the stocks pulled back. Although I did build substantial holdings in my winning trades, I still observed my trading rules by scaling into those trades. I was also willing to risk the amount of money I had calculated for my stop loss. However, when I lost on my one momentary blunder with Netflix, I had gotten way too overconfident and felt invincible, so I did not scale in slowly.

WHY? The best way I can explain is since I had several wins recorded in the books, I felt I could not lose! In fact, I had not made a bad trade in well over three or four months or more prior to my blundering loss. However, I lost my focus and wandered outside of the **neutral zone**. The fact is, I forgot that I was still just a goldfish, and I foolishly swam right into the mouths of the hungry sharks.

I know I said earlier that the sharks don't want to waste their time with a goldfish, and that is still true. Sharks are not interested in eating you or me for lunch for that matter; however, if you swim directly into an investing shark's mouth as I did, that shark just might oblige and take a bite out of you for an easy meal—just as they did me.

Remember, nothing is wrong with being a confident goldfish. The danger lies in being outside the neutral zone and becoming a foolish, **overconfident** goldfish by swimming directly into the shark's mouth for an easy meal by abandoning your trading rules and trading plan.

I will admit to loving calculating numbers and matching my odds against others as I always feel I have an advantage. I am generally able to calculate my risk/reward, and I like my odds to win more times than I'll lose.

I have always been fascinated by the World Series of Poker (WSOP). Poker tournaments are held throughout the world all the time, but each summer thousands of men and women from around the world gather to match their skills against one another in a large WSOP poker tournament held in Las Vegas. The players have a chance to win millions of dollars. If you are playing against one of these seasoned pros, they will likely eat you alive—unless you get lucky.

Many of the best poker sharks who gather at this summer poker tournament are well known by their competitors. Some of my favorite players are Daniel Negreanu, Phil Ivey, and Antonio Esfandiari. If you were to play against any one of these poker sharks, you had better be on your "A" game or you will be eaten alive. Unlike BIG sharks in the trading world, poker sharks are out to gobble up their opponents—one delicious bite at a time!

I enjoy watching these poker players calculate their odds and match wits against one another. I don't know how I would do if I played poker, but I do enjoy the strategy and mindset involved. I liken this strategy somewhat to the stock trading world in which I play.

What is most interesting to me about the game of poker is that even the very best players can make bad decisions and blunder at times at the poker table—even lose their edge. The key to their success is that they always find a way to rebound even if not in the present game or tournament. They will get refocused and enter another game or tournament at a later time and win then. Thus, they can continue playing the game as they know it because they know they will get back on their winning ways.

I want to merge these thoughts on poker with stock trading...

I felt the same type of confidence **soon** after my momentary blunder. Notice I used the phrase **soon** after—not *immediately* after. I did, however, laugh and tell myself quickly after that experience, "I will learn from this mistake and be an even better trader in the long run."

Becoming a BIG shark investor/stock trader one day is always a possibility. In fact, I would say if you dedicate your time to improving yourself, and that goal is something you really desire, then it is entirely possible. However, for most people, learning to be a confident and wise goldfish will offer you a life beyond most people's wildest dreams. That game is the one I choose to play.

I want to continue summing up the lessons I learned from my momentary blunder with Netflix.

My first big mistake was forgetting who I am. I am a confident goldfish, and I can swim successfully with the sharks and reap nice profits. I got careless and swam right into the shark's mouth. How? First, by taking on too large of an initial position to start with, and I lost my edge. Although I might have had the ability to trade with a little larger account now than I once did, I still do not have anywhere near the buying power and or staying power of the big wealthy sharks. I should have started with a much smaller position and scaled in slowly—like I do in all my transactions, including my BIG winnings trades. Unfortunately, I did not think about losing or perhaps I should be so bold as to say that I didn't even consider the fact I could possibly lose money on this trade as I had been winning on almost every trade.

My next mistake was in losing my confident edge. Confidence does not mean you always believe you are going to WIN. No, a confident edge also involves trusting your abilities and trading rules, knowing where you are willing to take a calculated loss and playing good defense when you're wrong. I did not play the good **defense** that I addressed in chapter 7.

You must always be careful to follow your trading rules—knowing and abiding by your stop loss, exit, and entry points for profit and loss. When (NFLX) started to go down, I suddenly realized I had not decided on a set stop limit order. As I said, I did not even consider the fact that I would lose money on this trade, so I figured, *Why bother?* What a big mistake! I also did not anticipate that this stock would drop as fast and as far as it did because it had been riding so much momentum going up. And I even knew that with stocks anything is possible.

I had simply grown way too overconfident since I was on such a BIG win streak, and I wandered outside the neutral zone. I finally set a stop limit order, but then I kept adjusting it downward as the stock continued to drop more and more, and finally it was too late...yet another difficult lesson learned!

I should have NEVER adjusted my stop loss down. When you adjust your stop loss, it should only be up or set a trailing stop. You should never be lowering your stop loss, trying to save yourself from being stopped out like I did. Once the stock had reached a certain level of no return, I was too far upside down, and then I was **drowning**. I simply had to take a sizable loss as I had no confidence in the trade any longer and feared even more loss. Note: *a goldfish should never drown in the water!*

If I would have just determined what I was willing to risk in the first place against what I felt I could gain, I would have started by taking a much smaller position and set a stop limit order immediately after I initiated my position. Then I would have been just fine. I still would have lost money on this trade as it dropped far beyond what I could have possibly calculated, but I would have been stopped out much sooner and kept my losses at a minimum.

I was reminded by my momentary blunder that I had developed my trading rule for a reason! I had created a rule that specifically reminds me that I am taking on a smaller initial position for a reason. That reason is to lower my risk exposure if a stock takes a sudden drop like Netflix did shortly after I initiated my initial, and I might also add—way too large of a blundering position.

I should mention that I do take on higher risk and much larger positions in certain situations. When I feel the risk/reward is well in my favor, I take a larger position. But, of course, nothing is ever guaranteed. I normally use a 7-percent loss to calculate my stop limit order and a 7.5-percent price target gain. However, I will often stretch that to a 10 to 12 percent loss for a stop limit and as much as 10 to 20 percent or more for a profit gain at times.

However, I always discipline myself to start out with a smaller initial position—even when I feel confident the stock will likely make a nice run up and not pullback. If I get a pullback, then I add more and build up a sizable position in the stocks I know well and like the risk reward potential.

I thought of a good analogy I learned as a young boy when I attended a gun safety course. I remember the trainer taught us to handle every gun as if it were loaded at all times. Even when we were absolutely 110 percent confident that it was not, we should still handle the gun as if it were loaded.

The same principle applies to stock trading. Always handle a stock as if it could go off quickly in the opposite direction you expect—even when you are 110 percent certain it won't. I follow this rule now by initiating a smaller position regardless of my confidence level that it will do what I think it will do.

I also make certain I know what my loss tolerance is versus my win potential on every single trade and immediately set my stop limit order. In staying with the gun analogy, I believe it's like making certain you have the safety on. I have been at this stock trading game a long time, and it took me many years to formulate my trading rules and gain familiarity with the stocks in my baskets in order to trade with more confidence and take on some larger risk at times. However, I still stay in the neutral zone and stick to my trading rules.

When you develop a positive winning mindset and adhere to a solid set of trading rules, you'll be able to scale up your risk potential as well, but you must always stay in the neutral zone and remain focused. I have chosen to scale down somewhat to a slightly smaller account since that momentary blunder. I have also moved more of my portfolio funds into dividend and growth stocks and some money into other types of investments simply to keep myself in check and my portfolio proportionally balanced.

I still take a higher risk on certain trades in stocks I've successfully traded many times over a period of time when I see huge upside potential, and I measure my loss potential versus gain if things do not go my way. But I remind myself often to treat the stock as if it could go off in the wrong direction at any time.

Thankfully, since that momentary blunder, I have gotten myself back on track and continue to work diligently at staying in the neutral zone. I know now that I must stick with my trading plan, follow my trading rules, and keep a positive winning mindset as I move about swimming in these shark-infested waters.

You can confidently swim with the sharks too, but you must always be aware of your surroundings and not make yourself easy prey. Know your risk/reward before you ever go into a trade and handle the stock with caution by taking a smaller position when you initiate the trade.

When you develop a positive winning mindset, you can confidently swim with the sharks and not fear for your life. Yes, when you're able to swim in the big tank with the sharks, the experience can be fun. Knowing you are in dangerous waters is thrilling, but if you're armed with a positive winning mindset and a solid set of trading rules, you can experience incredible joy and success when you remain calm and confident. If you stick with your plan, dreams of winning BIG can and do come true.

> *"When you invest, you are buying a day that you don't have to work."*
>
> —Aya Laraya

> *"Rich people believe 'I create my life.' Poor people believe 'Life happens to me.'"*
>
> —T. Harv Eker

CHAPTER 9

Small Basket of Goodie Stocks

This chapter will be important to your success in trading stocks, so I suggest you get a cup of coffee, tea or your favorite beverage and get ready to take some notes!

As I have eluded to in previous chapters, the one key I employ in maintaining my positive winning mindset is by following my trading rules and trading a small basket of extremely **familiar** stocks. I will explain this "basket" in greater detail, but first I want to address what I feel is a BIG mistake made by most stock traders.

If you've ever conducted any Internet research looking for that next BIG winning stock, then you have inevitably come across advertisements with the following messages:

- "Buy these 3 stocks now for HUGE profits!"
- "Use this stock chart setup for trading success!"
- "The best 5 stocks to day trade now for big gains are only a click away!"
- "Make $5,000 per month trading these HOT stocks."

The inexperienced trader will often click on the link or ad, provide their email address, and try a few of the stock picks. Perhaps they will make a little money or lose a little money, and then the search continues for the next BIG stock. Inexperienced and unsuccessful traders are always searching for the next best trading gizmo or stock to trade.

If you want to win at this stock trading game and beat the market, then you must STOP chasing the next best thing and stick to trading good stocks that you know extremely well through careful study of the market.

"How do I get to know them so well?" you might ask.

You get to know the stocks you swing trade well by simply watching them closely and repeatedly swing trade only your favorite stocks.

I want to explain what I mean by a small basket of familiar "goodie stocks." At the most, I only have 10 to 15 stocks in my trading basket, and I watch and regularly trade those same stocks for long periods of time. However, in a year's time, I may only swing trade four or five of those stocks in my basket, but I do swing trade them multiple times throughout the year.

I continue to watch all the stocks in my basket, but I develop relationships with my favorite stocks that I trade time after time for consistent gains. It's important to note that I am primarily speaking of my swing trading basket, but I do have some stocks that I day trade as well when I am looking for a change of pace and conduct a little day trading.

It's no secret that I love watching sports like football, basketball, golf, etc. In fact, when football starts up each fall, it's almost like Christmas Day for me! I especially love when college football teams start playing. I feel the same way when women's college basketball gets underway as well each year!

The one common denominator in these sports is that certain teammates play and execute better together than others. In football you will see a quarterback pass to his favorite receiver more often than he does to any of the other receivers. This is true at any level, but compiled stats in professional football prove this fact.

- Quarterback Joe Montana and Receiver Jerry Rice — 67 touchdowns
- Quarterback Brett Favre and Receiver Antonio Freeman — 67 touchdowns
- Quarterback Peyton Manning and Receiver Reggie Wayne — 76 touchdowns

These quarterbacks and receivers were so successful together because they worked together for a long time and executed the same routes and passes over and over again in practice. Their consistent practice led to success in the games. However, the real secret was the familiarity they had with one another. Peyton Manning knew about where Reggie would be, and if he delivered a decent pass to him, then chances were better than not that Reggie would catch the ball for a successful completion.

The same type of chemistry can be seen between basketball players as well. Prior to the Covid-19 shutdown that prematurely concluded the 2019/20 college basketball season, one of the deadliest combinations in women's college basketball consisted of Sabrina Ionescu and Ruthy Hebard of the Oregon Ducks. Those two ladies had perfected the pick-and-roll combination so well, they just knew where each other would be before it even happened at times. Their rhythm and harmony was beautiful to witness.

I would like to correlate these sports examples to trading stocks. When you develop a favorite trading relationship with certain stocks, you can get to a point where you just know about where they will go, which allows you to execute with better precision.

Going back to the sports analogy, did Peyton and Reggie complete every pass between them? No, of course not, but they were still champions! Did Sabrina and Ruthy execute perfectly every single time? No, of course not, but they were champions. Unfortunately, they never got the opportunity to prove if they could finally be national champions as the tournament was cancelled, but I believe 2020 would have been their year!

You can rightfully surmise that you will not win every trade even on stocks you know and love to trade often. Just like losing occasionally in any type of sports is part of the game, so is losing occasionally in the stock trading game, but if you will develop a relationship with some of your favorite stocks and trade them over and over, you will have more success in completing successful trades versus trying to learn new stocks all the time or always searching for the next best trade.

As a rule, I am always doing some research on new stocks I hear about, so I will occasionally drop a stock and add a new one to my swing trading basket to watch, but I like to find quality stocks and learn how they trade to the best of my ability over time. Then I trade them over and over based on previous patterns, etc. Again, in keeping with my rules, I only choose stocks I understand and ones that have business models with a history of success.

I can assure you that if you spend hours and hours watching the same stocks every single week and learning how they trade on good days and bad days (like athletes practice the same plays repeatedly), then you can develop a positive winning mindset because you will learn to be very good in a small area of expertise. Continually trying to pick new winning stocks over and over is difficult. You will find some good trades and you'll find some losers, but ultimately in the end, you'll likely end up losing more than you win.

I also love the game of golf, and I often watch golf training videos online to learn new techniques to improve my game. I heard a golf instructor say that many golfers practice for hours and hours, but they never get any better. The reason why they never get any better even though they spend hours practicing is because they practice wrong.

The same can be said for stock traders. They can practice trading strategy after trading strategy and still lose money. Why? Because they continue to practice the wrong strategies over and over. One poor strategy is constantly trying to find winning stocks and always trying new tips and techniques. The trading game is not rocket science! You find a winning stock by watching good stocks for a long period of time and building a winning relationship with those stocks.

I have one stock, Dollar General (DG) that I have traded repeatedly for positive gains for a while now. I became aware of Dollar General when I first started noticing Dollar General stores being built all around the area where I was living. I looked them up and found that DG was trading around $78 per share at the time.

I put DG in my watch basket and watched this stock for a while as it slowly worked its way up higher and higher. After studying it for several months, I finally made my first swing trade investment in Dollar General (DG) @ $132 per share. I made a few thousand dollars on my first swing trade and continued to watch it go up and down on a nice steady pattern.

I have day traded DG stock at times as well, but I mainly use it for swing trading. I have had some small losses at times, but my profits far exceed my losses. I would be so bold as to say that I have probably made more money trading this one stock alone over the past couple years than many stock traders have made in their entire trading careers, chasing all those so-called *winning* stocks.

Yes, you really can make an incredible income trading only a small basket of stocks over and over again. I should further mention that I also hold a long position in Dollar General in another investment account as well. So, like the other stocks in my trading baskets, I watch this stock daily. DG is not a stock for some traders as it can be a somewhat boring at times, but it has been one of my steady bread winners over the past few years.

There is no magic to making money with stocks and developing a positive winning mindset. It really is as simple as choosing good companies, learning their trading patterns over time and following your trading rules. Take the time to learn about the company's products and/or services and what makes them tick. Obviously, you want stocks that have a nice upward momentum.

Stocks never go up in a straight line. They will always go up some and then readjust down or pull back and then go up more and pull back down some. At times the market will control the stock on BIG down days or bad weeks with massive market self-off's, and everything goes down regardless of the quality of the company. However, if you have been trading a certain stock for a long time as I have been with DG, then you can take advantage of those dips and pull backs as you better understand what you are trading rather than always trying to trade unfamiliar stocks.

So, what about (NVAX)? If you recall, this stock was another one of my big winners, but I started trading it fairly soon after I discovered it rather than watching it in my basket for a long period of time like I normally suggest, before taking an initial investment. Okay, fair question! I am always doing a little research for possible opportunities for stocks I may want to add to a day trading basket, swing trading basket or long-term growth and dividend basket. The reason I was researching (NVAX) was because the Covid-19 pandemic was unfolding, and I knew there would likely be some golden opportunities in the biotech industry.

I am not the smartest guy on the block, but at the time, it did not take a genius to figure out that the market was buzzing about biotechs' desperate search to find a possible vaccine for Covid-19.

I started researching biotech companies—just like everyone else was doing at the time who had a finger on the pulse of the market. In doing my research on Novavax (NVAX), it seemed that this stock was one that was well worth the gamble and ready to possibly soar—but not because of the Covid-19 potential alone.

I initially invested in (NVAX) because it had other marketable vaccines in the pipeline like NanoFlu that was due to announce stage three test results at any moment. All indications were that those results would be positive. However, the Covid-19 rush happening at the time sent this stock soaring to the moon. Thankfully, I was onboard the spaceship!

As I have also mentioned, I had invested in many biotech companies and other higher risk stocks in the past. However, long before I had some big winning streaks, I had been developing my trading rules and my positive winning mindset. So, I believed LONG before I ever hit some really big wins that I would hit those big wins. I did not know the specifics of when, where, what, how or any other details, but I knew I would eventually make it happen if I stayed disciplined.

Yes, I just knew I would be successful at this stock investing and trading game if I kept believing I would be successful. Again, as I have already explained, I liken it to the same way I approach life by living the *Quick-Charge Concept*! I continue to believe I will hit even more BIG wins in the future, and eventually I'll go on from this life to heaven. That will be my final BIG win and by far the biggest win of my life!

I have already outlined how to find good stocks in chapter three. The good ones are not hidden. Yes, it would be nice to buy into any company's stock in its infancy and hold it until it's a BIG powerhouse company making you a multi-millionaire. I have owned several potential million-dollar winners…if I had only held them long term—I would have made multiplied millions.

I have been very fortunate to record some big winners, but that million-dollar stock trade has yet to happen for me in one trade! However, I believe it is still very possible since I do have a nice basket of long-term growth and dividend stocks that I hold, and I plan to hold for many years to come. I do believe some of the stocks I currently hold and watch now have million-dollar trade potential. Don't worry; I'll reveal those stock symbols to you in the pages ahead for you to consider adding to your watch list or portfolio as well, but so many more BIG winners are yet to be discovered!

So, if you need to go back and re-read chapter three again to learn about choosing good stocks for your baskets, then by all means, do so. I will note that my day trading basket is a little different, but I still try to find companies whose business model I understand for my day trading basket as well.

Do your research and find some good stocks that you understand, but only put a few good ones in your trading basket. Learn all you can about those companies and how they trade on a daily, weekly, monthly, and annual basis. Once you learn how these stocks trade on a regular basis, then start by taking small positions and build up your account by executing small wins over and over again as you build your relationship with those stocks. Then build on this success to make even more profits… Trust me, this information is invaluable!

> *"Earn as much as you can, save as much as you can, invest as much as you can, give as much as you can."*
>
> —John Wesley

> *"Money is something we choose to trade our life energy for."*
>
> —Vicki Robin

CHAPTER 10

Long Term Investing Basket

When it comes to a positive winning mindset, I feel it is most important when you're swing trading and or day trading as you always need to be focused and follow a strict set of trading rules. However, over the years I have added more and more to my portfolio of long term divided and growth stocks baskets. I feel this addition has also helped me gain a winning mindset as I watch that account and those stocks grow over time.

I am hopeful that one day soon the dividends and long-term growth stocks will provide a nice semi-retirement for me. Yes, I did say semi-retirement. I can't imagine retiring all together as I love trading stocks, writing books, coaching others, and tuning a few pianos. However, I look forward to taking more time off to play golf more often and possibly travel some in the near future.

I strongly encourage you to find some good companies, become very familiar with them and then buy a few shares of stock that pay a nice dividend. Then find a good stock or two that you feel has good long-term growth potential.

You will want to look for companies you know and understand what they sell and/or the services they offer. However, when you are investing in a stock for longer term, I would also suggest checking several other aspects of the stock such as P/E ratios (Price to Earnings), news, dividend payouts, analysis, earnings, etc. Many good resources can be found online for learning about buying long-term stocks, but if you stick with the good companies that I will cover in another chapter, then you should have a good chance at success.

When you purchase stock in a company for a long-term investment, you should be thinking in totally different terms from when you are swing trading. You are not looking at the short-term gains or losses. When you take a position, you are buying these stocks to hold for several years. You should buy a stock and be willing to accept its ups and downs with the belief that five to ten years or more down the road, this stock will have been well worth the ups and downs it may experience.

You should always be looking to add to these holdings year over year. Being able to see your money grow will help you develop a positive winning mindset. Everyone wants to get rich quick, and I have had some very good fortune by hitting some big wins over the years. I have been at this game for a long time, and I have built and modified my portfolio and trading rules over the years—not over days or weeks.

My suggestion is to choose only a few stocks and not try to put a bunch of stocks in your growth or dividend portfolio. In my opinion, I would say no more than three to five different stocks. Then when one of those stocks takes a dip or pulls back, add a bit to them.

Again, there is no magic formula in my opinion on how to build a good basket portfolio of dividend and growth stocks. Just keep it simple. Choose good companies that either have a good record of paying their dividends for your dividend portfolio and stocks that make sense for long-term growth for stocks in your long-term growth portfolio basket.

I should mention that although I do have stocks in my growth and dividend baskets that I've held long term, I also find some good swing trades and/or day trade opportunities within that basket at times as well. Because they are stocks that I have held for a long time I am extremely familiar with how they react in good and bad market times as well. So, when they take a big plunge due to a market sell-off related drop, I will often buy more shares and then sell some when they go back up to capture a little up-front profit. Then I might re-invest that profit into one of my best dividend stocks or add to my swing trading account balance.

I remember hearing Warren Buffet once say that he got a bit giddy when the market had a big pullback selloff or correction because it is like finding all your favorite stocks on sale. Many people dread a big correction or pullback, but when you invest in quality stocks by major companies, those stocks have always had a good record of rebounding to greater heights. So, when they are on sale, then add a little more to the basket and watch them pay you in nice returns in the future as they go back up.

I think it might be important to talk about stop-loss protection in this basket as well. I do not tend to put stop losses on my big stocks that I am holding for a long-term investment until I have some larger profits built up in a certain holding. I realize there could be some major corrections in the market at times, and the stock could drop as much as 30 or 40 percent or even more.

If I hear that the company is possibly in trouble, that would likely change my mind on a certain stock holding, but I don't want to be stopped out of a stock that I am planning on holding for years simply because of a market correction. If you have no intention of selling the stock except for occasionally trimming profits, then why set a stop limit?

The exception to this rule is if you have a large profit to protect. At that point you should be reducing your position size some to realize some profits and/or set a trailing stop to protect against a market reversal to save your profits.

It's quite important to understand that you will not be trading these stocks unless you see a good opportunity to buy on a correction and ride some of those shares back up. Then trim your position to take some profits. You are mostly just buying these shares and then tucking them away in the portfolio to hopefully watch them grow over years and years.

I highly recommend one important tip with dividend stocks. Set all of your dividend stocks to automatically reinvest the dividend payment back into the stock each time they pay. This method will allow your number of shares to continually grow larger and larger; thus, your dividend amount grows as well.

Your online brokerage firm should offer this reinvestment option and will reinvest the dividend payments for you automatically. Once you set the stock to reinvest, then the brokerage firm where you hold your account will purchase the additional shares for you with the payments from dividends on the stock and place them into your account. You do not need to do anything once this option is set up. On some stocks you'll get an even better return as they will reinvest at a lower price than the current price, allowing you to accumulate even more shares since you are keeping your money in the company and not taking anything away. It's a beautiful setup.

The next extremely valuable tip when it comes to dividend investing is to look at the bigger picture. Just because one stock has a larger dividend payout over another company does not always mean the larger dividend payout will pay you more return over the long run.

Many stocks that might have a much smaller dividend payout over another stock may actually have much more growth potential. So, in the long run, if you add up the amount of dividend you receive plus the amount of growth that you get on your investment over time, then the overall combined returns may be a much greater amount overall on the smaller paying dividend stock.

These investing strategies have greatly helped me develop my positive winning mindset. On days when things do not go so well, I can look at my growth and dividend baskets and know I am still doing well. At times when these stocks drop significantly as well and it hurts to see them so low, I just add to them and watch them rebound over time to even greater heights.

If you are just getting started, then you can gain confidence by simply choosing a few good dividend stocks and growth stocks. Using the rules for picking a good stock and putting a few shares in the basket will build your confidence simply by starting a good portfolio of stocks. If one of your stock holdings takes a nosedive that is not based on the company's having major problems, then simply add a few more shares and let them grow.

The last point I want to address on a growth basket of stocks is trimming your position or profit taking. There will be times when a stock or the market in general has become so overbought or overheated that it is inevitable that your stock or the market might make a correction regardless of the direction of the market whether it be bull-or-bear market conditions.

If you are up a good percentage of profit in a certain holding, then trimming the position is always good and selling a few shares (maybe 25 to 50 percent or so of your holdings) to capture some profits. When the stock does correct (and they will), then you have saved some profits and can buy back more at a lower price with that extra cash.

Trust me, if you hold a stock for long term, it will correct at times. When it does, simply buy back in. If the stock is up big, then it's important to only trim a percentage of shares and not exit the position all together—unless you set a trailing stop or you simply want to close out the stock and you believe it's really going to take a plunge. By keeping a percentage of the shares in your portfolio basket, you always have your finger on the pulse of the stock.

> *"Value stocks are about as exciting as watching grass grow, but have you ever noticed just how much your grass grows in a week?"*
>
> —Christopher Browne

> *"A big part of financial freedom is having your heart and mind free from worry about the what-ifs of life."*
>
> —Suze Orman

CHAPTER 11

The Million Dollar Swing Trade Secret

Swing trading a stock is by far my favorite type of trading strategy and where I play the game the best. I do enjoy day trading to a degree, but the game plan can become somewhat intense at times; therefore, I much prefer to stick with swing trading the majority of the time. For those who still may not be clear on what a swing trade is...

Swing trading is a style of trading that attempts to capture short- to medium-term gains in a stock (or any financial instrument) over a period of a few days to several weeks. Swing traders primarily use technical analysis to look for trading opportunities.

I do not claim to be a technical stock chart guru. Chances are you may not be a technical stock chart guru either, so you might be wondering, *what is the big million-dollar secret to making money with a swing trade?*

You already know the BIG million-dollar secret that I revealed to you in chapter 9. The secret is simply to watch the stocks you are swing trading for a long time and only trade your favorite stocks rather than trying to make winning swing trades jumping from a new stock to a new stock all the time. If you are constantly searching for new stocks to swing trade, then you will always be unfamiliar with the stocks you trade. That lack of familiarity makes it nearly impossible to stay in the neutral zone and focused on winning.

The strategy that I am teaching in this book is to know your stocks extremely well and build winning relationships. Once you have a small basket of very **familiar** stocks, you can then trade those same stocks multiple times throughout the year as you find a number of good swing trade opportunities.

As you trade your favorite stocks over and over again, you will develop a relationship with those stocks like quarterbacks who throw to their favorite receivers. I swing trade some of my favorite stocks five, six, seven or more times per year. You will learn to notice a stock's tendencies and patterns in good times and bad times, and you will have had the opportunity to review the analyst reviews, follow the news coverage, and hear the commentary from others who cover the stocks you trade.

When I take a position in a familiar stock, I tend to already know about how far the stock has dropped in the past before it goes back up. I also know about how much it has gone up before it pulls back as well. I still do not have a crystal ball to tell me the future, and I have no way to really know for absolute certainty where that stock will go next or if the entire market will take a sudden change in direction up or down. Therefore, I **must remain disciplined** to stay in the **neutral zone** and follow my **trading rules**. But I do have an edge over other competitors playing the game based on the fact that I am so familiar with the stocks I trade and how they trade.

If there is a market sell off, causing one my favorite stocks to drop while I am currently in a swing trade with that stock, I do not panic or feel the need to jump off the rollercoaster ride. I can stay calm and enjoy the ride. If I do not get stopped out of my position and the opportunity presents itself, I can buy more shares and ride it back up for even more profits.

When I am in a swing trade, I will likely hold my position in a stock anywhere from a few days to three or four weeks. Occasionally, I'll stay in a swing trade for two or more months in some cases as I seek to make anywhere between $500 to as much as $5,000+ per swing trade that I enter.

Perhaps I need to quickly clarify my profit goals here. I have been at this stock trading game for several years now so although I suggest that you start slowly and take small positions as you build up your account. I have followed those same rules and principles, starting slowly as well, but I now have the luxury to play the game by taking positions that are small, in essence, compared to my account size. Although they are much larger position sizes than when I first started my trading journey, they are still small positions based on my account size.

When I now take a "small" position, that may be 207 shares or 477 shares or 1007 shares, and so on... These positions allow me to make a much higher profit margin when my swing trades work out because the favorite stocks that I trade often go up 7 to 10 percent within a few days to a few weeks at times. Of course, they can drop this much as well, so my losses can be much greater when a trade does not work out, and I get stopped out.

My hope is that you will also build up your account over time and one day enjoy the same results that I now do. By being armed with a solid set of trading rules and a positive winning mindset to start out with, hopefully you will attain your account goals much quicker than I did.

Continuing on... Most of the example trades that I have used in this book for learning purposes are based on starting with a much smaller account size and building it over time so you can increase your trade amounts. However, in this chapter, I will be using examples based on having a much larger account balance with which to trade.

I feel that creating a vision or a goal for the future and helping you see the real possibilities of what you can achieve and expect down the road is very beneficial. To do so, I cannot emphasize enough that you must stay disciplined and stick with a small basket of stocks that you trade over and over. Now that I have set the stage, let's continue with my tutoring lessons.

I usually hope to purchase enough shares to make my initial $500 to $1,000 profit goals should the stock reach my projected target price. However, if the stock pulls back a bit after my initial purchase, then I will add more shares and give myself the opportunity to make even more money climbing the ladder toward my $5,000+ profit mark. Of course, I am also setting myself up to lose more money as well, but I have already precalculated my risk/reward before ever initiating the trade.

If the stock continues to go up after I take my initial partial position, then I just ride my initial position up until it reaches the price target that I felt it would reach, and then I sell. I do not make as much profit as I had ultimately hoped since I never got in all my shares on the ride up. If it drops or pulls back some after my initial purchase (which happens more times than not), then I will add more to dollar average down, giving myself the opportunity to make more profit.

On successful swing trades, I normally make anywhere between $500 to $2,000 profit on my winning swing trades. I do occasionally make $3,000 to $5,000 and much more on some of my better swing trades, but I have also lost that much on some trades when they did not rebound or just plain did not work out.

Perhaps you're asking this question: "HOW can I lose money when I know the stocks I trade so well?"

The answer is really quite simple: although we may know the stocks that we swing trade extremely well, we still cannot change the fundamental truths of trading. One of those fundamental truths is that ANYTHING can happen.

There are times when I am in a swing trade with one of my favorite stocks, and I have accumulated a rather large position of several hundred shares or more. But then the entire market sells off rapidly, my stock goes down with it and stops me out. The fact is, you will make money, and you will lose money at times. Stocks will go up, and stocks will go down. They always have, and they always will. But if you will employ a disciplined trading strategy, you have a much better chance at winning the game!

I want to share an example of a larger swing trade in detail so you get an idea of how to enter and exit a swing trade.

Suppose XYZ is currently trading around $103 per share. You have watched and traded XYZ for a long time in your basket, and analyst reports put out a new price target of $115+ in the future. So, you calculate a 7% stop loss limit from the intended entry price of $103 where you plan to enter the trade, which is roughly $95. You then check the support level on the chart to see if the stock could find support before hitting your stop loss point of $95.

Next, you check to see how much a 7.5% increase from the intended entry price of $103 per share will be, which is about $110 per share. That amount is below the analyst PT of $115, so this is a potentially good swing trade.

Earnings are coming up in a few weeks for this stock, and since you have watched this stock trade numerous times coming into and through earnings reports, you know that earnings have been good the past few times on this stock. All indications are that earnings will be good again. You also know that in times past XYZ usually runs up into earnings regardless of what direction it goes after earnings. How do YOU know all this? I'm sure you already know the answer, but it's because one of my trading rules is to know what you trade so YOU have followed and traded this stock for a long time, learning its patterns and tendencies.

For those who may be skeptical of the viability and methods or rules discussed in this book, I want to play devil's advocate momentarily. Couldn't you simply study a stock for a little while, check the past earning reports and also check the past history of the chart and the price action over the last few times it traded into earnings? Yes, of course.

Couldn't you also look back over several analyst reports and view news from the past to see what the experts are saying about a stock? Yes, you can do that too; in fact, you should do all these things before you ever choose to put a stock in your trading basket to watch.

HOWEVER… Yes, I capitalized this word to get your attention! However, if we go back to the quarterback and receiver combinations I addressed, there is something important to note. ALL of those quarterbacks and receivers were superstars. Each one was great in his own right at playing his respective position. They had a winning combination that worked well for them because they were very familiar with the teammate with whom they worked. If they were to jump from team to team, that chemistry would NEVER happen or be the same even though they are all great players.

Although you could learn a great deal about a stock in a short period of time by doing diligent research, the principles I teach are all about **building relationship** over time with the stocks you trade. Once you apply these rules and principles to your trading game, this dynamic will change the game and how you trade stocks.

Two weeks or so prior to the company's announcing earnings, calculate how many shares you would need to purchase to make at least $500 to $1000 profit should the stock reach the $110+ price target. Based on its current price of $103 per share and your projected price target of $110 per share based on a 7.5% increase from your initial $103 per share entry price, that is a gain of roughly $7 per share. Therefore, you would need to purchase roughly a total of 145 shares (145 x $7 gain = $1,015 profit gain).

I want to share what I call a silly little aspect of my personal swing trade purchase strategy that has absolutely nothing to do with how you should trade or anything I have ever learned. I happen to like the number 7, so I always put in initial orders like 57, 77, 177, 407 shares, etc. If I do buy an even number or another odd number of shares when adding to a position, I still keep my total holding to something with a 7 in it. I know it sounds silly, but my consistency in using the number 7 is one of the small things that I like to think gives me a winning edge when I swing trade.

Since we stay with the rule never to purchase our whole position to start, you will initially start by initiating a position with half of the shares you will need. Let's say you purchase 77 shares. Remember, I always purchase in amounts with a 7 in the number of shares because 7 is my thing—not something you need to adopt, but for this exercise, I'll use this method.

Now, your goal is to secure at least 145+ shares total into the trade, but you will only take on about half of that position with your initial purchase. In this case, you would purchase about 77 shares as mentioned to start with at a limit order price of $103 per share.

If, after you purchase the initial 77 shares, the stock runs up from $103 to $110+ price target without any pullbacks below your initial $103 purchase price, then you will not make your $1,000 profit goal since you would only own 77 shares. But you will still make a nice profit of just over $500 on the trade.

However, if the stock pulls back after your initial purchase with relatively light volume, then you will likely add more shares.

This is always a call you must make as you watch what's going on in the market and your feelings on the stock you're trading at the time as you've watched it react over time. If you do get a pullback, then at this point, you will likely hold enough shares to make your $1000+ profit or more when the stock reaches your price target of $110+.

When studying the chart, there are areas where you know the stock could be in trouble if it falls below what is called *support,* so you will be out of the trade because of your stop limit. There are also areas that are called *resistance* that you know might be difficult for the stock to get through; however, your price target may or may not be beyond that point, so you need not be as worried about resistance.

There will be times when your trades will not work out. You will lose larger amounts of money when you get to a level where you can trade in larger amounts. If you limit your losses and maximize your gains, you will win at this game and enjoy much bigger profits.

When I swing trade, there are times that I am simply after an even smaller amount of profit or at least what I consider a small amount of profit of $200 to $300 on a quick swing trade, but I determine my intentions before I ever make a trade. The reason I will switch to this smaller profit strategy is that the market has become somewhat choppy or inconsistent. At times the market will have an up day and then a couple down days, and then the market rebounds for a couple of days, but then it becomes very erratic again. I like to get in and make a little profit and then get back out.

My thought is that I hope not to be in the trade more than a few days to catch a small run up. As I mentioned, this may be based on the market's being somewhat unstable or perhaps other factors involving the stock itself, but the reasoning is often because I do not trust being in the trade for more than a few days, but I am still after making some profit and growing my account. So, I set my stop loss and profit levels a bit tighter at a 2% loss to 2.5% profit or a 3% loss to 3.5% profit, etc. I like to think of it more as a mix between day trading and swing trading.

With most of my normal swing trades, it takes two or three weeks and even more at times to reach my projected price target. Depending on the number of shares I accumulate during this time dictates my total profit, of course. When I am after smaller profits or perhaps, I should say quicker profits, then I will set lower price targets.

Many times, I will sell my shares and the stock continues to run up, so I miss out on more profit, but I achieved my objectives. If you do this often enough, you soon discover that it builds a strong positive winning mindset, and the quick profits are very rewarding when you do it multiple times per month with your favorite stocks.

As I already mentioned, I will not get into much of the technical side of trading as you can get too caught up in this aspect. It will often cost you more money because you convince yourself the stock will do this or do that based on what you THINK you saw in the chart.

The first main key is simply to KNOW your stocks extremely well and develop a winning relationship. Yes, just know the stock well and watch it trade over a good period of time through good-and-bad market conditions. Then control your emotions and stay in the neutral zone, follow your trading rules, and rely on your positive winning mindset. Then simply trade your favorite stocks over and over again.

If you will simply follow this secret ingredient to successful swing trading, it will give you an edge over 90 percent of the other traders who jump from new stock to new stock all the time in hopes of making their fortunes with a swing trade.

Yes, my friends, that really is the million-dollar secret to making huge profits with swing trades.

> *"The investor's chief problem—even his worst enemy—is likely to be himself."*
>
> —Benjamin Graham

> *"Risk comes from not knowing what you're doing."*
>
> —Warren Buffett

CHAPTER 13

Is It Luck or Skill?

As you might have noticed, I chose *lucky* number "13" for this chapter and topic. As I recounted earlier in this book, I have had some very big wins, but were those big wins *luck* or *skill*? I would say good trading is definitely based more on skill, but some elements of luck or good fortune do go along with the skill as well.

Since the time of my really big wins, I have heard people comment that I really got *lucky* to be in Novavax (NVAX) and Dollar General (DG) and some of the other big stock trades I have made. Well, I guess that supposition is true to a point, but I really do not see any wins as merely a *lucky* series of trades or stock picks.

I liken it more to how professional athletes talk about all the missed shots in a basketball career or all the strike outs in their baseball career. Over time, they also had many home runs or game-winning shots. All of those athletes were successful because they put in the work and had a positive winning mindset along with a disciplined set of rules and practice regimens that I am sure they followed every single day to reach the successes they did—just as I do and teach with trading stocks.

When you enter a trade, you are doing so based on research and knowledge that you have acquired on a stock from watching it trade over a long period of time. This part is skill—*not* luck. Furthermore, following the rule of not taking on too large of an initial position and scaling into a swing trade slowly is also skill—*not* luck.

However, when a stock you are trading takes a sudden big gap up and you make a huge profit, this part can be attributed to some luck and/or good fortune. I do believe your skill placed you in that position. I consider my biggest wins to date as a combination of both skill, luck, good fortune, and God's blessing in my life.

Skill requires doing my research or due diligence and watching DG trade for several months before ever taking my very first initial position. I did take a position on NVAX much sooner, but I had already familiarized myself with Biotech trading. Based on this knowledge and what I had discovered about this particular company, I felt I had a good chance at success (skill).

Next, I took smaller positions to initiate those winning trades (skill). I scaled into the trades with more and more shares as they pulled back (skill and good fortune). Then NVAX gapped up for some huge profits (some skill, luck, good fortune and a blessing from God).

Perhaps I should also mention for anyone who is crunching the numbers: if you are wondering how I made such a big profit when I usually set a 7.5% profit price target goals. I do not always use a 7% loss or 7.5% price target profit. I will often stretch this to 10% to 12% loss, and 10% to 20%+ price target profit at times on stocks I feel have much more potential. However, in the case of my big wins in NVAX, the stock gapped up well beyond any price targets I would have set long before the market even opened. The good news often came after the close of the market the day before. I was definitely fortunate to make considerably more profit than just a 7.5% to 15% profit goal.

Perhaps also important to point out is that when you set a profit goal, you are not actually placing a sell order like you do with a stop limit order to protect loss. Although you have a profit goal price target in mind where you will sell a stock for profit, it may jump up well beyond your profit goal, so you make much more on the trade.

I continued to swing trade NVAX stock in the same manner for several more months (skill and good fortune). It continued to go up and up, giving me wins over and over again (good fortune mixed with skill and God's blessing). I have successfully traded DG for huge profits over the past few years (both skill and good fortune).

I do feel very fortunate that I got in on the good side of the ride up for Novavax (NVAX) at the time, and I definitely feel the win was a combination of skill, luck, good fortune, and a huge blessing from God. Unlike the person who buys a lottery ticket and wins a great deal of money, my wins were NOT the same type of *luck* at all.

Many people say that stock investing and trading is a form of gambling, and I do feel there may be some similarities if you only buy a stock and hope to get lucky. But a good stock trader is always disciplined to follow a strict set of trading rules, making calculated risks and not gambling! I knew that I could potentially lose money on any of those trades, but fortunately for me, they ended up being winning trades. I feel relatively certain that many people probably did lose a lot of money on those same stocks during the exact same time I made a lot of money.

I know the same is true for my big wins in Dollar General (DG). I first started watching this stock because I saw many Dollar General stores being built in my area. I figured if the company was building so many stores in my area, then very likely this was happening all around the country as well. I started following (DG) for several months before I ever made my first initial swing trade (skill).

It is very good fortune that Dollar General stock has continued to climb from the first time I started trading it, but the stock has also experienced some large dips down due to overall market sell-offs. As I watched and studied the stock, I noticed it has always rebounded quickly, so I took full advantage of this knowledge. However, I am sure that not everyone who has traded this stock has had the same success stories or knowledge of its tendencies that I do.

Exactly the opposite happened on my blunder with Netflix (NFLX) when I took a bad loss. I am sure that many traders made a lot of money while I lost a chunk of money on that same stock. My loss was the result of my being undisciplined and wandering outside my neutral zone, which culminated in losing my winning edge. The market is always a battle of traders winning and losing, which is why keeping a positive winning mindset and a solid set of trading rules is so essential. You can keep the advantage in your favor.

If I had stayed in the neutral zone and followed my set of trading rules and positive winning mindset which keeps me grounded and focused, then I would have never had the momentary blunder on (NFLX). I very well might have lost some money on that trade, but I would have minimized the damage. However, I simply lost focus and broke my trading rules. Neither skill nor luck is involved; it is simply not having your head in the game.

In the end, I believe that we create our own *luck* by being disciplined enough to stick to our trading rules and positive winning mindset. Call it what you want, but I sincerely believe successful traders reach their level of success by using wisdom and skill coupled with blessing more than they will ever rely on luck or gambling!

> *"How many millionaires do you know who have become wealthy by investing in savings accounts? I rest my case."*
>
> —Robert G. Allen

> *"It is not the man who has too little, but the man who craves more, that is poor."*
>
> —Seneca

CHAPTER 14

Cash Is King

One extremely valuable lesson that I have learned over the years is to always keep some cash on the sidelines. I always have stocks sitting in my watchlist baskets that I want to take a small position in whenever I see a big drop in the market. I also like to keep some cash on the sidelines to dollar average down when one of my long-term growth stocks or dividend stocks takes a bit of a dip.

I simply cannot express how vitally important it is to always keep some cash reserves in your account for golden buying opportunities as your account size grows. Remember, the two influencing factors to the stock market are greed and fear.

I almost titled this chapter “Don’t Dread the Red.” Before I developed my trading rules and other aspects of my overall trading philosophy, including staying in the neutral zone, I used to dread red-market days. I often avoided the market on days when I would wake up and see the DOW down 400 points and the NSDAQ down 100+ points or more.

However, once I developed my trading rules and started to build good relationships with my stocks to learn them extremely well, I learned to appreciate the buying or shopping opportunities presented by these red down days.

Think of a delicious homecooked meal that you prepared yourself or perhaps someone you love prepared for you. The first stage before you could enjoy that delicious meal would have been to purchase or harvest the food. The second stage would have been to prepare and/or cook the food to create the meal. Then **finally** you were able to enjoy the meal.

When you see deep red days where the market is down and you know your stocks well, you can see these days as being like harvesting or going shopping to buy the ingredients you need to enjoy a nice meal later. The second stage then is to monitor the stocks you just purchased as you would clean, cut, dice, slice, and then cook your meal as you dollar average down when the market continues to go into the red. Eventually the market goes up, and at this point, you are cooking or baking the meal until it is done so you can enjoy that delicious meal.

Therefore, you always want to have cash on hand to go shopping to buy the ingredients or, in this case, the stocks. You can then prepare the food or build your position in a stock. You can watch the various dishes cook until you can eventually enjoy the meal you prepared by building a nice position in a stock you know well.

When you sense fear in the market, that is usually a great time to be looking for buying opportunities. If you discipline yourself to build a healthy cash reserve, then you can take advantage of these opportunities and be richly rewarded. Also wise is to have cash on hand when you find good opportunities in swing trades that might pull back and allow you to take a larger position. Again, if you know a stock well and have a good sense of what is happening in the market, then it could be a great time to add and make larger profits.

As I have stressed repeatedly, it is so important never to go all in on a stock or even on several stocks using all of your reserve cash. I will admit that I have had many times when I am so tempted to want to enter a position by buying more of a certain stock to initiate a position in my swing trading basket when I am almost 99.9 percent certain the stock is ripe and going to pop up for a nice gain. Many times, my hunch proves right. However, I must remain content in knowing that I was right as I watch the stock go up—even though I am not holding a larger position.

I will still have my half position so I do not entirely miss out on the nice run up by taking a smaller starting position. I only miss out on making more money on that swing trade as I must stay disciplined never to overextend myself and use up all my cash reserves. I MUST abide by my trading rules to avoid another blunder.

One thing that has helped me stay disciplined since my blunder with Netflix is to put my set of rules near me or out in plain sight to keep me from stepping outside the lines. Just because I have learned to be a disciplined trader and have developed a positive winning mindset does not mean that I am not tempted to break the rules at times. Unfortunately, I do get out of balance and leave my neutral zone at times. Sometimes it costs me, but most of the time I catch myself and get back on track quickly.

Obviously, I must keep myself in check. At times, I will admit the needle on my emotional meter starts pointing too far left or too far right. However, I know in order for me to remain successful, I must always stay in the neutral zone and be very disciplined. I have learned that it is by far the most successful way to trade.

You will have times when a stock will pop up just as you felt it would, and momentarily, you may feel some regret that you did not trust your instincts and buy more. However, be cautious of being persuaded or influenced into thinking that the next time you will just trust your gut and buy more shares, ignoring the trading rules. If you do this once or twice, inevitably you are playing with fire and setting yourself up for a blunder at some point like I had with NFLX. If you do not stay in the neutral zone with your emotions, you will become just like 90 percent of the other traders who cannot seem to figure out why they never really make any money trying to trade stocks.

You may have stocks where you have a decent profit, but it has not reached your price point. So, you continue to hold only to see the entire market have a big correction and sell off. In this case, you watch all of your profits quickly disappear with it. However, when a stock sells off but does not stop you out, then you will be thankful you still have cash on hand and have the opportunity to buy more shares at a lower price.

You've probably heard the saying: it takes one to know one! I know a rookie or a losing stock trader when I meet one and listen to him talk about his trading strategies. After all, I used to be just like those losing traders for many years as well!

Let me share what I believe is the best way to discipline yourself to keep some cash on the sidelines. You should divide your portfolio into an investing budget just like you would do with a home spending budget.

First, allocate 50 percent of your account funds to swing trading only. Of that 50 percent, you will have about 40 percent working at any given time; you should discipline yourself to hold back the remaining 10 percent. On occasion a great opportunity presents itself in a swing trade, so you can break into that 10 percent when you want to buy more shares on a good dip. If you have all 50 percent of those funds working, then you must hold off from doing any more stock purchasing for this basket.

Next, allocate 30 percent of your funds for long-term and dividend stocks. This budget is fairly easy to maintain as you are not trading these stocks. You can simply set those stocks aside or possibly even create a separate account.

Next, allocate 5 percent to high-risk speculation stocks for higher risk plays. These are funds you are basically gambling with a bit—for lack of a better term.

The remaining 15 percent of your cash should be on the sidelines waiting for those big dips and golden buying opportunities.

Setting a disciplined budget will help you from going all in on a stock and losing more than you should have. Up until I decided to divide up my account funds, I simply bought and sold stocks with little thought to what I was doing. I could not believe how foolish I was all those years not to manage my money better.

> *"A lot of people with high IQs are terrible investors because they've got terrible temperaments. You need to keep raw, irrational emotion under control."*
>
> —Charlie Munger

> *"Compound interest is the eighth wonder of the world. He who understands it, earns it. He who doesn't, pays it."*
>
> —Albert Einstein

CHAPTER 15

Investing in Baseball Cards

I realize my book is primarily about trading stocks, but I also want to include some additional pointers about investing. You can invest your money into many venues outside of the stock market. In fact, I feel building your net worth by diversifying some of your portfolio is very important and shows wisdom. Investing some money into other mediums outside of stocks can also bring a nice return as well.

Many people choose real estate as their alternative investment means. Others choose to invest in fine art. Many people will put a portion of their portfolio into gold and silver. Some high-end investors might invest in classic cars or higher-end cars like Ferrari, Lamborghini, and Porsche. Collectible coins or stamps is another interest for some investors. Another approach to investing is in shoes! Some people buy and sell sports shoes like stocks. All of these investments can be very lucrative over time—if you know what you are doing.

As I go outside "of the box" in this chapter looking at alternative investment venues, I would like to introduce you to one of my favorites (outside of stocks). I would like to briefly delve into the fascinating and **highly profitable** world of baseball card collecting and investing. If you have no interest in alternative investments or specifically in baseball card investing, by all means, feel free to skip this chapter. However, you might discover that investing in baseball cards can potentially provide you with an amazing return on your money. I do hope you'll stay with me and learn why I feel investing in baseball cards can be a very solid investment strategy for long-term financial growth.

Possibly you may not even be aware that baseball cards have become a major investment venue for many investors around the world today. Over the past several years, baseball cards and sports card collecting in general have become a very lucrative and active industry for many people seeking alternative investments with some astonishing returns.

I started buying, selling, and collecting baseball cards, basketball cards, and football cards as a hobby back in the late 80s, but in the early days, collecting them was mainly a fun hobby for me. I often bought and held cards in my collection for a few months to a year or two, and when they increased in value, I sold them and bought more cards.

I knew cards like a Mickey Mantle rookie card or a Michael Jordan rookie card were increasing in value, but those cards were already expensive even when I first started collecting cards in the 80s, but I really never saw baseball cards as a viable investment alternative until a couple of years ago.

Like many of the good stocks I have bought and sold over the years, I now wish I still had many of the vintage baseball cards and basketball cards that I bought and sold in the early days of my interest in sports card collecting. Unfortunately, I sold off most of my early card collection that I acquired.

In the past 10 to 15 years, sports card investing has been gaining in popularity. Many sports cards are popular to collect such as baseball cards, football cards, basketball cards, hockey cards, golfing cards, etc. Non-sports cards as well have made their way into the records books for the amounts they have sold for at auctions. If sports cards are not your thing, then perhaps there is a non-sport card you might find worth investing into.

My main focus for now is on baseball cards, so I will use that platform as the premise for the argument that you should consider investing a portion of your portfolio funds into baseball cards as well. Baseball card collecting and investing gives me a tremendous amount of joy and satisfaction. Baseball cards are a very solid investment for anyone to consider whether or not you enjoy the game of baseball. Ironically, baseball is one of my least favorite sports to watch, but my favorite sports cards to collect.

I have bought and sold tens of thousands of baseball cards, football cards, and basketball cards on eBay since 1998. As I mentioned, I unfortunately sold off most of my card collection from my early years of collecting. I no longer partake in the "selling" of cards on eBay these days, but I did start actively "buying" cards on eBay in 2017 and continue to buy them on eBay as an active investor as of this writing. My main investment portfolio is in professionally graded vintage baseball cards from the 1950s to 1970s.

I only invest in professionally graded baseball cards. I tend to favor cards graded by PSA (Professional Sports Authenticators), but I also buy some cards graded by SGC and Beckett. These graded cards have been professionally authenticated and given a grade or a score based on many factors that determine the card's overall condition and quality.

A card with a grade of PSA 10 is the cream of the crop, and if you're lucky enough to own some of the top baseball stars from the 1950s and/or 1960s in a PSA 10 grade, it is likely that your card is worth a small fortune in today's baseball card market. I do not own any PSA 10 gems myself, but many of the Hall of Fame stars of this era in a PSA 10 grade can sell into the hundreds of thousands to millions of dollars.

Let me give you some quick examples of baseball card investment returns you could have expected if you had started investing in cards years ago. The following is only a small sampling:

These numbers are from 2008 to 2020 are based on only a $10,000 investment. The S&P 500 had an ROI (Return on Investment) of 102% = $10,200 return profit. Baseball cards during that same period had an ROI (Return on Investment) of 264% = $26,400 return profit.

Based on the above example, baseball card investing would have given you more than double the return of the S&P 500. Many of you may not be able to afford any of the high-grade Mickey Mantle cards that will run into the tens of thousands and hundreds of thousands of dollars: however, many good cards of slightly lower grades are still available, as well as other stars that are very worthy investments.

One of the keys to success in baseball card investing is to buy as high a grade a card as possible and look for the best quality in a certain grade. Not all grades are equal.

I mainly focus my attention on cards with a grade of PSA 3 to PSA 8 for most of the cards I invest in. However, I do search for the best-looking PSA 3 to PSA 8 in their class. I will often pay a higher premium to purchase the best quality PSA 3 that I can find of a certain player. There might be five PSA 3 cards of the same player and brand for sale on eBay all having the same exact grade of PSA 3, but one of those PSA 3 cards will often clearly be a better-looking card than all of the others even though they all carry the same PSA 3 grade. I believe investing in these premium-graded cards will continue to grow in desirability and value over time.

I still keep most of my investment money in the stock market as I enjoy buying and selling stocks, but I do take a portion of my profits and invest them in baseball cards every year. I feel that baseball cards are an excellent investment alternative and one you should consider putting some of your portfolio funds into as well.

If you are interested in this investment alternative, the following is a quick basic primer on where to start. I really feel there are two investment classes for investing in sports cards whether it be baseball, basketball, football or any other sport.

Investor Number One: The Wealthy Investor

If you are fortunate enough to have a considerable amount of cash on hand, then the first strategy would be to focus on the rarest cards you can find of Hall of Fame star athletes from the 1930s to the 1990s, including players like Babe Ruth, Mickey Mantle, Joe DiMaggio, Ted Williams, Ernie Banks, Willie Mays, Jackie Robinson and others.

Investing in premium high grades of these cards will rule out 99 percent of investors as many of these cards can run in the tens of thousands to hundreds of thousands of dollars, and even into the millions. Highly valuable baseball cards and other sports cards sell into the millions of dollars at auctions every day. Like I mentioned, the high-dollar sports card game is not likely one that most investors reading this book can play but is a viable and very lucrative investment vehicle for the wealthy investor. I would be remiss not to mention this alternative.

If you have the financial means to invest hundreds of thousands or even millions of dollars into sports cards, you could likely double or triple your money in a reasonable period of time. Yes, the sports card market is just that lucrative!

Investor Number Two: The Average Joe Investor

The second strategy is to invest in mid-grade cards PSA 3 to PSA 8 of stars from the 1950s to early 1970s. However, I suggest you stick to the best in class for the grade you invest in. If you can afford to invest in cards valued in the $500 to $1,000 price range, I think that will be your best investment. I feel the $500 to $1,000 graded cards will double in value much more quickly than a $5,000 to $10,000 card. This price range currently will get you cards with a PSA 2 to PSA 5 grade for the mid stars and some of the major stars in their later years.

As I have already mentioned, I would stick with only PSA, SGC, and Beckett graded cards.

If you can afford it, focus on baseball players like Mickey Mantle, Willie Mays, Ted Williams, Jackie Robinson, Roberto Clemente, Hank Aaron, Nolan Ryan, and Sandy Koufax, who are some of the key players and most collectible from the 1950s to 1960s era.

You may not be able to afford the rookie or second year cards for many of the players I have listed, but you can find some nice cards during their careers that are still very desirable and more affordable. However, if you can afford to invest a few thousand into a second- and third-year card in a good solid grade for any of the players listed, I would grab them.

If you would like more information on investing in baseball cards or sports cards in general, then I invite you to reach out to me on tommyturner.com, and I'll be happy to speak with you about a more detailed investment strategy.

> *"I put two children through Harvard by trading options. Unfortunately, they were my broker's children."*
>
> —Jason Zweig

> *"If you want to be a millionaire, start with a billion dollars and launch a new airline."*
>
> —Richard Branson

> *People calculate too much and think too little.*
>
> —Charlie Munger

CHAPTER 16

Buy and Hold These Stocks for Life

I have bought and sold thousands of shares over the years as I learned the ropes of playing the stock trading game. Just like I mentioned with some of my most valuable baseball cards that I sold, I wish I still had some of the stocks that I bought many years ago as well when getting started. Unfortunately, I sold those early investments many years ago as well.

If you are just starting out with your stock investing and trading career, then you might wonder what stocks you should possibly consider buying and put them away for many years to come. This is obviously a very wide-open question and, depending on when you're reading this material, there is no right answer per se. As I work on this chapter, no one really knows what the stock market will look like in 10, 15, or 20 years from right now.

If I had to suggest some potential names of stocks that I would look at owning long term, I would say there are obviously many to consider. The following is a short list of my favorite stocks that I currently hold and will hold in my portfolio for many years to come.

Tesla Inc. (TSLA)

Tesla, Inc., formerly Tesla Motors, Inc., designs, develops, manufactures, and sells fully electric vehicles and energy storage systems, as well as installs, operates and maintains solar and energy storage products. The company operates through two segments: automotive and energy generation and storage. The automotive segment includes the design, development, manufacturing, and sales of electric vehicles. The energy generation and storage segment include the design, manufacture, installation, and sale or lease of stationary energy storage products and solar energy systems to residential and commercial customers, or the sale of electricity generated by its solar energy systems to customers. The company produces and distributes two fully electric vehicles, the Model S sedan and the Model X sport utility vehicle (SUV). Tesla also offers Model 3, a sedan designed for the mass market. It develops energy storage products for use in homes, commercial facilities, and utility sites.

Tesla is high on my list and one I personally hold in my portfolio basket of long-term growth stocks for the future. Tesla will likely have some ups and downs, but this stock could seemingly be huge in several years. Actually, it already is huge. Tesla stock has been on a rapid rise up and is currently trading at just over $2,000 per share as of this writing, but it will split 5 to 1 very soon, so I will wait to add more shares to my position. By the time you are reading this chapter, I will hopefully own several more shares of Tesla (TSLA)! I am optimistic it will do very well over time.

Dollar General (DG)

Dollar General Corporation is a discount retailer. The company offers a selection of merchandise, including consumables, seasonal, home products and apparel. The company's consumables category includes paper and cleaning products (such as paper towels, bath tissue, and other home-cleaning supplies); packaged food (such as cereals, spices, sugar and flour); perishables (such as milk, beer and wine); snacks (such as candy, cookies, and carbonated beverages); health and beauty (i.e., over-the-counter medicines and personal care products); pet supplies and pet food, and tobacco products. Its seasonal products include decorations, toys, batteries, stationery, prepaid phones and accessories, and home/office supplies. Its home products include cookware, craft supplies and kitchen, and bed and bath soft goods. Its apparel products include casual everyday apparel for infants, toddlers, girls, boys, women and men, as well as socks, underwear, disposable diapers, shoes and accessories.

Dollar General is another of my favorite long-term holdings in my portfolio and a stock I have traded for HUGE gains over the past few years as well. If conditions allow, I will hopefully continue to trade Dollar General for many more years. Dollar General also pays out a small dividend, which is a little added bonus. I feel the dividend combined with the growth return will make this stock an excellent long-term growth investment. This is one of my prize holdings in my portfolio and swing trading basket.

Apple Inc. (AAPL)

Apple Inc. designs, manufactures, and markets mobile communication and media devices, personal computers and portable digital music players. The company sells a range of related software, services, accessories, networking solutions, and third-party digital content and applications. The company's segments include the Americas, Europe, Greater China, Japan and the rest of Asia Pacific. The Americas' segment includes both North and South America. The Europe segment includes European countries, India, the Middle East and Africa. The Greater China segment includes China, Hong Kong and Taiwan.

The rest of Asia Pacific segment includes Australia and the Asian countries not included in the company's other operating segments. Its products and services include iPhone, iPad, Mac, iPod, Apple Watch, Apple TV, a portfolio of consumer and professional software applications, iPhone OS (iOS), OS X and watchOS operating systems, iCloud, Apple Pay and a range of accessory, service and support offerings.

I feel Apple is a company that will always find ways to innovate and stay competitive. I see this as another excellent stock to buy and set aside for many years to come. I currently hold this stock, and it has been on a rapid rise lately, trading at $498.95 as of this writing and will also split 4 to 1 soon. I will obviously own much more of it after the split. Apple also pays a small dividend, making it even more attractive to own long-term.

Invitae Corporation (NVTA)

Invitae Corporation utilizes an integrated portfolio of laboratory processes, software tools and informatics capabilities to process deoxyribonucleic acid (DNA)-containing samples, analyze information about patient-specific genetic variation and generate test reports for clinicians and their patients. As of December 31, 2016, the company's products consisted of assays totaling over 1,100 genes that could be used for multiple indications, including hereditary cancer, neurological disorders, cardiovascular disorders, pediatric disorders and other hereditary conditions. The company offers panels for a range of hereditary conditions in cancer, cardiology, neuromuscular, pediatric and rare diseases. The company focuses on genetic testing, genome network and genome management. The company offers full gene sequencing and deletion/duplication analysis as a standard for all of its tests. The company holds interests in AltaVoice, a patient-centered data company.

Invitae is a company that I think could pay back big rewards over the long term, but it is a riskier play. It does not currently pay a dividend, but I feel it is an attractive growth stock to buy and set aside for a long-term growth stock investment.

Quanterix Corp. (QTRX)

Quanterix Corporation develops ultra-sensitive digital immunoassay platform and tools for life science research and diagnostics. The company offers single molecule array (Simoa) platform, which uses single molecule measurements to detect protein biomarkers. The company is also focusing to enable and develop novel therapies and diagnostics to facilitate in healthcare for earlier detection, monitoring, prognosis and, ultimately, prevention of disease. Simoa focuses on research and clinical testing applications and significantly advances enzyme-linked immunosorbent assay (ELISA) technology, which is capable of unprecedented protein detection sensitivity. It also focuses on research and diagnostics for brain injuries, heart disease, cancer and other infectious diseases with its technology. The company offers Simoa HD-1 analyzer, which is an automated immunoassay platform with multiplexing and custom assay capability.

I recently took a nice position in QTRX and will continue to add to my position in this company. I plan to hold this stock for several years as well. I believe the returns could be extremely high over time. It is one that you should be prepared for some big swings up or down over time and play it accordingly. On big drops, add more, and if it goes way up, trim a little.

I believe Quanterix Corporation stock (QTRX) could be one of those "I-TOLD-YOU-SO" winning investments, but of course, I could be wrong; only time will tell.

AT & T Inc. (T)

AT&T Inc. is a holding company. The company is a provider of telecommunications, media and technology services globally. The company operates through four segments: communication segment, WarnerMedia segment, Latin America segment and Xandr segment. The communications segment provides wireless and wireline telecom, video and broadband services to consumers. The business units of the communication segment includes Mobility, Entertainment Group and Business Wireline. The WarnerMedia segment develops, produces and distributes feature films, television, gaming and other content over various physical and digital formats. The business units of the WarnerMedia segment includes Turner, Home Box Office and Warner Bros. Latin America segment provides entertainment services in Latin America and wireless services in Mexico. Viro and Mexico are the business units of the Latin America segment. The Xandr segment provides advertising services.

I hold this stock long-term mainly for its nice dividend that has paid out consistently for years. I feel it is a stock that will continue to innovate and pay its dividend.

AGNC Investment Corp (AGNC)

AGNC Investment Corp., formerly American Capital Agency Corp., is a real-estate investment trust. The company invests in agency residential mortgage-backed securities on a leveraged basis. Its investments consist of residential mortgage pass-through securities and collateralized mortgage obligations (CMOs) for which the principal and interest payments are guaranteed by a government-sponsored enterprise, such as the Federal National Mortgage Association (Fannie Mae) and the Federal Home Loan Mortgage Corporation (Freddie Mac), or by the United States Government agency, such as the Government National

Mortgage Association (Ginnie Mae) (collectively, GSEs). Its agency securities include agency residential mortgage-backed securities (Agency RMBS) and to-be-announced forward contracts (TBAs). Its Non-Agency Securities include credit risk transfer securities (CRT), non-agency residential mortgage-backed securities (Non-Agency RMBS) and commercial mortgage-backed securities (CMBS).

I have held this stock in my portfolio for several years. It pays a nice monthly dividend and has continued to pay those dividends month after month. There is no guarantee they will continue to pay a monthly dividend or even keep a dividend at all, but I have found it has been a good stock to hold and one I feel is worth holding long term.

As promised in an earlier chapter, here are some other ticker symbols that I hold and ones for you to consider investing in for the long term...

AMZN, ILMN, CRSP, RMD, MSFT, FB, NKE, ROKU, TWOU, O, SQ, PRLB, and NVAX.

This list of tickers are only a few good suggestions of stocks that I feel have great potential. I hold all of these stocks in my portfolio for various reasons. Some are for long-term growth investments, and I hold some for dividend investment. I watch all of these stocks closely and use several of these stocks to swing trade and/or day trade as well.

I have given you a short list of some potential winning stocks for you to consider and ones I currently hold in my portfolio. There are many more good stocks to consider of course, but this list gives you a peek into my personal portfolio holdings and stocks that I feel will be good investments for many years to come. Of course, no one really knows for sure what will be the next BIG winners and losers in the future, but I am confident that some of these companies will be great stocks to hold for 10 to 20 years or longer.

> *"If you owe the bank $100, that's your problem. If you owe the bank $100 million, that's the bank's problem."*
>
> —Old Proverb

> *"More people lost money waiting for corrections and anticipating corrections than the actual corrections."*
>
> —Peter Lynch

CHAPTER 17

Are You Married or Just in a Relationship?

I am sure the title of this chapter may be somewhat confusing in a book about stock trading and investing, but I can assure you this topic has everything to do with stocks, trading, investing and more.

What exactly do I mean when asking the question "Are you married or just in a relationship?" Well, I am referring to the type of investment or trade relationship you are committing to on a stock investment when you initiate a position. If you are only swing trading the stock, then you are, in essence, only committing to a short-term relationship with the stock. However, if you are initiating a position in the stock with the intentions of holding long term, then you are, in essence, committing to a long-term marriage relationship with the stock.

Many stock traders will initiate a position in a stock trade with the intention only to hold it short term in a swing trade. So, at that point, they are saying they are only in a short-term relationship with the stock and have no intentions of staying with the position long term, which would result in their being in a committed "marriage" relationship with the stock. However, at times, many traders often lose focus on what was supposed to be a short-term swing trade and make the mistake of staying married to a stock.

When trading stocks, you must always be careful not to have commitment issues with your trades. If you are going to initiate a short-term swing trade on a stock, then that is exactly what you should be doing. Before you initiate the swing trade, you should predetermine your stop limit, price target for profit, and entry point, and then execute according to the plan, knowing you're committing to a short-term swing trade relationship—NOT a marriage relationship.

Always be absolutely certain to execute the trade based on your set of plans that you have determined for that trade and not on a weak commitment to your rules. If you deviate from your plan, you will likely end up in an unpalatable relationship with that particular trade.

I am obviously being a little sarcastic in my tone in this chapter as I compare stock trading to human relationships, but some very close similarities really are true! If you recall in the million-dollar swing trading secret in chapter 11, I addressed the fact that the very premise of this book is about developing good relationships with your favorite stocks.

If you predetermine ahead of time that you plan to hold a portion of the investment long-term, then you may start with a swing trade, but continue to hold a portion of the position long-term. As I have mentioned a few times, I hold some stocks in my long-term trading basket portfolio that I also swing trade and/or day trade on occasion as well in another account. But I still continue to hold some shares of that stock in my long-term portfolio basket as well.

However, the point of this chapter is to make absolutely certain that you predetermine what your intentions are when you enter a trade relationship with a stock. Once you determine what type of relationship you want with the trade (long term or short term), then initiate a position and stay with that decision. It is usually a bad choice to enter a short-term swing trade relationship with NO thoughts or intentions of committing to a long-term marriage relationship, but then end up choosing to merely stay married to the trade. If you do this, then at some point you will likely "fall out of love" with the trade and lose money in the "divorce." And if it's a really bad trade, you stand to lose a lot of money when you "divorce" the stock.

The moral of the story is this: when you're only in a short-term swing trade relationship with the stock, then stick to that decision. Do not be influenced by fear that you should hold on until the stock recovers or perhaps get greedy, thinking, *it's going to continue going up and up*—after it has blown through your price target.

If your intentions are only a short-term swing trade relationship and you have no intentions of being married to a stock long-term, then accept your losses if you get stopped out. If the stock is at your price target, then take your profit. Don't end up married to a stock you are not in love with and committed to holding for the long haul.

If you initiate a position in a stock with the intentions of a long-term marriage relationship, then be committed to that relationship as well. If you hold a stock long-term, there is a very good chance it will go through some difficult rocky times. That does not mean that in the end the relationship is not a good one to stay with. Times will come when the stock will simply go through a difficult period or bad market conditions. Perhaps it's not increasing in value like you had hoped or at the pace you would like. Perhaps that is the time to show the stock a little love and add to the position instead of giving up and divorcing the stock.

While on the subject of relationships, I have a few more thoughts before wrapping up this chapter.

It's perfectly acceptable to just be "friends" with a stock as well. I have good longstanding relationships with some stocks that I have successfully traded many times for years. I am always clear on my intentions each time I initiate a trade with those stocks, and we get along just fine. Sometimes I lose some money, but more times than not because I have such a good relationship with these stocks that I watch in my trading baskets, things often work out very well.

I do have stocks that I have traded for a long time only as a short-term swing trade relationship, but I end up falling in love with the stock over time. Based on all that I learn about the stock, I now have a long-standing committed marriage relationship with them and plan to hold them for many years to come. One of my favorite stocks, Dollar General (DG) is one of those stocks that started off as a swing trade-only relationship, but over time I also became a long-term investor in the stock and also continue to swing trade it as well in another account.

As you may have cleverly deduced, my intention with this chapter was to have a little fun with a play on words or meanings when it comes to relationships, but also to show you exactly how closely related stock trading and investing is to real-life relationships. The fact is, investing and trading in the stock market is REAL life and involves REAL relationships, and you must be very focused and committed to your intentions. Never try to fool yourself or change your mind and deviate away from your trade plan and trading rules. Always be disciplined to stay with your rules and trade plan, stay in the neutral zone, maintain a positive winning mindset, and your stock relationships will all work out the way they are supposed to.

I also want to caution that simply because you are committed to all your rules and remain focused with your intentions with a stock trade or investment, that does not mean all your trades and investments will work out and make you money. They simply won't. However, if you stay the course and follow what I have outlined in this book, you will have a much better chance of success with your stock trading and investing career!

I felt I had concluded my thoughts on this chapter, but then I had one more quick thought that hit me that I want to record here. As I was driving to my office this morning, I was thinking about the committed relationship I have with the Lord, my children, and my friends. I thought about how blessed I am to have all the wonderful relationships that I do have in my life.

This thought reminded me that **no** amount of money will ever replace the love and joy I receive from my **relationship** with my Heavenly Father! No amount of success or money will EVER replace the love and joy that I have with my family and friend relationships.

There is not a winning trade BIG enough that you should ever chase after money as a replacement to the value you will receive from **investing** time with the Lord, your family, and your friends. These life relationships are truly what are most valuable and important! I don't know about you, but that little reminder gave me a *quick charge*!

> *"Games are won by players who focus on the playing field—not by those whose eyes are glued to the scoreboard."*
>
> —Warren Buffett

> *"An investor without investment objectives is like a traveler without a destination."*
>
> —Anonymous

> *"Don't work for money; make it work for you."*
>
> —Robert Kiyosaki

CHAPTER 18

The Neutral Zone

I have talked about the importance of staying in the neutral zone multiple times in this book, but I want to be absolutely certain that you really understand what I mean by this term. I also want to be certain you understand how it will benefit you when it comes to trading and investing in stocks.

The stock market will take you on many loops, turns, ups, and downs during the day, during the week, and certainly during a year. I equate this sudden extreme changeableness to a roller-coaster ride. As I mentioned in the introduction of this book, I have learned how to handle the emotional rollercoaster ride filled with the many ups and downs that come with trading stocks.

However, notice that I said I have learned how to **handle** the rollercoaster ride and **not** how to **avoid** the rollercoaster. We ALL must stand in line like every other stock trader in the world and hand our tickets to the Wall Street ride attendant so we can get back on the stock market rollercoaster ride every day when the stock market opens. You will eventually learn how to enjoy the ride and not be influenced by its ups and downs, twist and turns when you stay in the neutral zone.

If you have ever been to an amusement park and watched a rollercoaster filled with a bunch of people, you will see a plethora of different emotions and expressions on people's faces. You will see some people with big smiles on their faces and their hands are raised in the air as the rollercoaster quickly plummets downward toward the ground. Then you will see other people with their hands tightly clenching the rail in front of them with a look of horrifying panic and fear on their faces. These riders appear as if they are going to die as the rollercoaster plunges toward the ground!

Remember, all of these people are on the same exact rollercoaster ride, experiencing the same twist, turns, ups, and downs as everyone else. So, which person is right? Well, the answer is all based on each person's perception of what is happening at that moment. Please remember this analogy when it comes to stock trading and investing.

As I have stated frequently, I feel one of the keys to enjoying the stock market rollercoaster ride is to stay in the neutral zone and keep a positive winning mindset so you can enjoy the ride to success. However, staying in the neutral zone is not always easy, and I do admit, I get a little dizzy or scared at times. However, I quickly find my way back to the neutral zone so I can focus on what I am doing. These thoughts go hand-in-hand with the last chapter on knowing what type of relationship you're in with the trade.

So, exactly what is the neutral zone? Staying in the neutral zone simply means never to be fooled by the price action. Since the stock market is a rollercoaster ride, it is supposed to go up and go down, plummeting toward the ground at times and then climb back up, racing toward the sky at other times. However, you must not allow this ride to sway you from your trading plan and trading rules; you should not make emotional trade decisions. Let me continue to explain with some examples, but first you must understand **what** the stock market rollercoaster ride is really trying to do. The stock market rollercoaster will always try to scare you or provoke fear, causing you to sell too soon or buy too early. It will also try to influence you into being overconfident or even make you greedy by holding on too tightly to a trade, trying to get that very last penny.

However, you can get into the neutral zone by *not* allowing your emotions to be influenced by all the loops, ups, downs, twists, and turns in the market. You must step back and see things for what they really are—just a rollercoaster ride. Once you master this skill, you will have a much better chance of success. At times one of your really good stocks will take a dip down, but that is no reason to bail out of the stock—unless it hits your stop limit. Sometimes a stock is way up, which may be a time to trim and take some profits.

For example, I was recently in a swing trade with one of my stocks, and I decided on this particular occasion to hold my swing trade position through earnings, which is something I rarely ever do on any swing trade. However, holding or not holding a swing trade through earnings is not one of my steadfast trading rules. To me, it is more of a judgment call, and I usually recommend closing a swing trade position before earnings. Again, that is a call you must make as you get to know the stocks you trade.

Getting back to my swing trade… I held my position on this particular occasion through earnings because I fully expected it to go up to my price target right after earnings were announced. I felt the earnings would likely be very good; however, the stock dropped instead—but not because the earnings were bad. In fact, they were quite good as I had expected, but it dropped because they did not blow out their earnings as many had anticipated.

This stock has followed this same exact pattern in times past as well, so I was very aware this could possibly happen. By staying in the neutral zone, I did not allow my emotions and trade plan or rules to be swayed by this rollercoaster drop or change in direction. I chose to take advantage of this drop and added more shares for another ride up on this rollercoaster ride.

If I had allowed myself to get scared and bail out of this trade, then I would have been leaning too far toward the fear side and not be in the neutral zone. Of course, had it hit my stop limit price I would have been stopped out. It did not reach that point because I had set my stop limit a bit lower on this trade based on the fact that I knew it might drop more even on good earnings. Again, I knew this stock well—just like many others stocks I trade. I felt that even though it did not go up to my PT after the earnings announcement like I thought it would, I still felt it would go back up soon. Thankfully, it did. If I had been wrong and it did not recover and continued downward, then I still had my stop limit order already in place. I would have lost money, but that is just the way the rollercoaster ride goes at times.

Knowing a stock extremely well and observing its tendencies over time will help you to stay in the neutral zone and not be swayed by all the twist and turns on the market rollercoaster. I will admit that when you are in a swing trade, the rollercoaster ride can be a bit more confusing at times, and you can get somewhat dizzy when you go through some big twist and turns.

One way I know to help you understand this rollercoaster ride is by always remembering the Five Fundamental Truths of Trading Stocks that I have already shared in chapter six. The first truth: "Anything can happen" is important to remember.

If you think about it, when someone gets on a rollercoaster ride at an amusement park, they already know that it will go up and down and loop around or whatever, and yet, they are either excited or terrified by each movement that happens.

So, when you get on the stock trading rollercoaster ride, it should not come as any big surprise when the ride goes up or down or takes some twist and turns. Why? Because you already know anything can happen, and you have willingly taken on this rollercoaster ride by investing and trading stocks. So, why scream and panic when the market is plummeting toward the earth? After all, it has done that many times over the last hundred years and will do it again several more times in the future.

So, how do you put a smile on your face and enjoy the rollercoaster ride? When it is going down, you must wait until it starts an upward run and buy good stocks on "red days," i.e., when stocks are basically on sale. Anticipate the drops as well as the high spots. When a stock goes down in the red, then buy more or initiate a new position if you know it is a good company like the ones I have already listed in this book. If the market is going up green, then wait until it gets to a high point and sell or trim your position.

When I am in a stock for the long term, I am not tempted or influenced nearly as much by the ups and downs of the rollercoaster ride in the market. In fact, if one of my long-term holdings has a drop and I know the company is still strong, then I use that opportunity to add to my position with a smile on my face and my hands raised in the air with joy. When the stock has been on a nice run up and my profits are looking good, I may use that opportunity to trim my position a little and take some profits. All the while, I am still on the rollercoaster ride, but I am enjoying the rollercoaster's dips and turns for what they are. I use those red-day dips and green-day high points either to add to my position or trim if the opportunities present themselves.

I found a word of encouragement in my daily Bible devotional that I felt was fitting to this concept and would like to share it.

> Try TO SEE THINGS more and more from My perspective. Let the Light of My Presence so fully fill your mind that you view the world through Me. When

> little things don't go as you had hoped, look to Me lightheartedly and say, "Oh, well." This simple discipline can protect you from being burdened with an accumulation of petty cares and frustrations. If you practice this diligently, you will make a life-changing discovery: you realize that most of the things that worry you are not important. If you shrug them off immediately and return your focus to Me, you will walk through your days with lighter steps and a joyful heart. When serious problems come your way, you will have more reserves for dealing with them. You will not have squandered your energy on petty problems. You may even reach the point where you can agree with the apostle Paul that all your troubles are *light* and *momentary*, compared with *the eternal glory* being achieved by them.

Although this devotional may not appear to be related to trading stocks, I feel it is actually closely related. I felt this paragraph helps to explain my point for remaining in the neutral zone with the market as well. The times when the market is chaotic and many become fearful, you must remember that the market always goes up and down. You have to learn to enjoy the ride and shrug off the bad days by simply giving it to the Lord. You must realize that most of what worries you is not important, including a bad stock trade. This perspective will allow you to step back and not be influenced by the market's swings, dips, rallies and more...

When you remain neutral, focused, and disciplined to follow your trading rules, you are doing far more than 90 percent of the traders who never win long-term! If you can visualize a meter and seek to keep your emotions in the middle instead of being influenced by fear and/or greed like so many others in the market who put way too much concern into each tick of the trade, then you can better see the whole picture and not make the bad mistakes that so many stock traders make.

You will never make every trade perfectly, and there will be trades that you lose money on, but that's okay. You will likely be a bit terrified at times as well on the really scary rollercoaster stock rides, but step back and realize it is just a rollercoaster. When you know the ride goes up and down, then the ride can be much more enjoyable when you embrace it. But regardless of what is going on around you, trust the Lord and try TO SEE THINGS more and more from His perspective.

> *"Trading doesn't just reveal your character, it also builds it if you stay in the game long enough."*
>
> —Yvan Byeajee

> *"What the wise man does in the beginning, the fool does in the end."*
>
> —Old Proverb

CHAPTER 19

A Change of Plans

As we near the end of this book, I hope you have found some valuable nuggets to use in your trading and investing plan. Hopefully, you will follow the suggestions outlined in this book and develop good relationships with a nice basket of stocks to trade for many years of ongoing profits.

However, I felt I should touch on a few more important points as I begin to wrap up this book. As I re-read this manuscript numerous times and made small adjustments here and there, I felt mentioning the fact that there are some instances when I do have a change of plans and wander outside the lines is also important.

I am NOT saying that I wander outside my neutral zone. No, I am speaking of something totally different here! I ALWAYS work very diligently to follow my trading rules and stay within my boundaries and keeping myself in the neutral zone. So, what am I talking about when I speak of "changing my plans or wandering outside the lines"?

What I want to stress is something extremely important that goes along with getting to know your stocks extremely well as you develop winning swing trade relationships with them. I will at times adjust my profit and loss percentages on certain trades based on what I feel the potential profit and loss might be.

As you may recall from earlier chapter examples, my main targets are often set at a 7% stop loss and a 7.5% price target gain. At times, I might adjust that stop loss from 10% to 12% or so and my price profit target to 10% to 15% or even more above my initial entry price. I rarely ever set my price target above what analysts are projecting, but I will set my price target higher than a 7.5% on many occasions.

This decision is made based mainly on my feelings that the stock may be a bit more volatile or perhaps I feel it has a lot of momentum to go even higher than 7.5% above my entry price. In that case, I widen my stop loss and price targets.

Perhaps even more important is a change of plans for closing out a trade early. There are many times when I will close out a stock trade for a nice profit before the trade ever hits the price target that I had calculated based on the first initial entry price.

The reason why I may choose to close out a trade "for profit" early is when I have had the opportunity to build up a sizable position of several more shares than I originally planned due to the stock's moving up and down, but never getting too close to my stop limit or going too far up above my original entry price. When this happens, I may choose to close the trade early, but for even more profit than my original profit goal.

Let me illustrate with a quick example trade:

XYZ is trading at $135 per share. A new price target is put out by two different analysts who follow the stock and who give a price target of $165. You determine that you will make a swing trade with a goal to make $500 profit.

First you calculate what a 7% drop would be based on its current trading price of $135 ($135 – 7% = $125.55 or $9.45 loss per share).

Now you look at the chart and determine that there is good support above this price so that is a good sign. Next, you calculate what 7.5% above its current price at $135 will be, which is a price target of $145.13 ($135 x 7.5% = $145.13 or $10.125 profit per share).

So, in order to make a $500 profit, you plan to get about 50 shares in the trade (50 shares x 10.125 profit = $506.25).

So, you initiate a limit order of 25 shares (½ the initial position desired) at $135, and the order is filled.

You immediately set your GTC (Good Till Cancelled) stop limit order to sell 25 shares at a stop limit of $125.55. Then over the next couple days, the stock pulls back to $132.50 on light volume, so you add 25 more shares at a limit order of $132.50. This purchase lowers your overall cost basis down to $133.50 per share.

You will then edit your stop limit order number to 50 shares, but do not change the stop limit price. Then a few days later, the stock goes down a bit more to $131, but you still feel this stock is going to go up based on past performance you've experienced in other trades with this stock so you decide to add another 25 shares at a limit order price of $131 per share. This addition lowers your overall cost basis even lower to $132.83 per share.

Now you are holding 75 shares, and then the stock starts working its way back up as you had anticipated. Remember, your original calculation was to exit the trade around $145.13 or higher based on taking the first position of 25 shares at $135 and calculating a 7.5% price target, but since you've added several more shares, your $500 profit gain you were hoping for will be reached before the stock hits this original 7.5% price target of $145.13.

So, let's say over the next couple of weeks, the stock works its way up to $142.50 per share. This is still shy of the $145.13 that you originally estimated as a price target for this trade. However, let's check what your profit is based on the cost basis and number of shares so far. You have accumulated 75 shares with an average cost basis of $132.83 per share, and the stock is currently trading at $142.50. This represents a $9.67 gain. 75 shares x $9.67 = $725.25 profit!

Although it is not at the original price target of $145.13 you had set, you may choose to have a change of plans and close out the trade early for an even nicer profit than originally planned.

Depending on your feelings about a stock and the overall market, you might want to close out a trade early and take those profits off the table. You would mainly do this if you perhaps feel the overall market will go down or maybe you simply feel the trade you're in is getting a bit sluggish; therefore, you choose to take the money and run.

I will admit, there are times I make brilliant calls when doing this and the market sells off, and my stock takes a nosedive the next day after I have closed out the trade for a sweet profit. There are also times when I close out my position for a nice profit before it hits my original price target, but then the stock still continues to go up. It could have easily hit my original price target, but I must keep myself in the neutral zone and not beat myself up because I missed out on more gains.

On the opposite side of the scale, I rarely ever close out a stock early and take a loss before it hits my stop limit order, but on certain occasions you feel you're on the wrong side of a trade as the market changes or things come out about the stock that are not favorable. Although it does not stop you out, you choose to cut your losses rather than wait for the inevitable.

Of course, there are times when you will do this and then the next day all the news changes, and the market sentiment is all good again. Unfortunately, you realize you could have made a nice profit rather than taken a loss, but that is all part of the market rollercoaster ride.

Let me be VERY clear and stress again that I am not in any way suggesting you ever break your trading rules or wander outside the neutral zone. No! I am simply saying that there will be times when you make a change in your plans because you have too nice a profit in a trade to leave it sitting on the table. In that case, you should close out a trade and bank that nice profit. Or you sell for a loss because you just feel the trade has no chance of rebounding, so you reduce your potential losses.

It's important to understand that the percentages I use of a 7.5 % gain or a 7% loss to calculate my price targets and stop loss points are not part of my trading rules. These are simply percentage calculations that have worked well for me, so I am suggesting you consider using these same guidelines as well. Since they are not set-in-stone trading rules, you can adjust them for each trade, and I often do.

Again, I do not recommend closing out a trade for a loss too often as it is usually best to just wait until you're stopped out. After all, you made the decision going into the trade that you were willing to lose the amount you calculated, so you set the stop limit order. But taking profits before they hit the original price target you set is one practice I would suggest doing on occasion—if you feel it may not reach your original price target, and you have a nice profit already sitting on the table.

> *"Beware the investment activity that produces applause; the great moves are usually greeted by yawns."*
>
> —Warren Buffet

Conclusion

> *"Learn to work harder on yourself than you do on your job. If you work hard on your job you can make a living, but if you work hard on yourself, you'll make a fortune."*
>
> —Jim Rohn

Although stock trading and investing have been the main focus of this book, I feel that the discipline to continually investing in *yourself* is vital to anyone's success in life and in trading stocks as well.

A few years ago, when I created the *quick-charge concept*, I developed what I like to call my "**Secret Sauce Formula**" for success. This set of disciplines and practices has literally changed my life, and I believe a similar formula will do the same for you as well.

Your "Secret Sauce Formula" will likely be different from mine. I developed my *quick-charge concept* coaching program around this formula concept, and now I help my clients to develop their own personal secret sauce formulas. But I want to give you a quick glimpse of what the secret sauce formula looks like.

Secret Sauce Formula

The **Secret Sauce Formula** is your personal regimen of **daily disciplines**, that will become your personal **Secret Sauce Formula** to which you must adhere daily. There should never be a day off. Your personal secret sauce formula ingredients may change over time, but you must create a formula that works for you personally and begin applying it to your life every single day.

The best way to understand how your **Secret Sauce Formula** will help you is by seeing it as a **toolkit** that you will carry with you through life. By applying a daily set of disciplines (**Secret Sauce Formula**), you will gain the wisdom, knowledge, strength, and skills you need to achieve whatever goals and/or dreams you have set for yourself.

My Personal Secret Sauce Formula: **"9.7"**

I. Make my bed.
II. Prayer
    1. Devotional reading
III. Speak positive words into my life.
    2. Express gratitude and thankfulness.
    3. Inspire others.
IV. File ideas, quotes, articles, videos, jokes, book clips.
V. Research.
    4. Listen to podcasts; watch educational and inspirational videos.
VI. Think.
    5. Ask questions (God, myself and others).
    6. Listen.
VII. Read.
    7. Bible, inspirational books, articles and blogs.
VIII. Laugh often.
IX. Journal my personal account of each day.

Each person will likely have a different mix of ingredients for his or her Secret Sauce Formula. As you can see, I have 9 main ingredients and 7 sub-ingredients that I focus on for my Secret Sauce Formula "9.7." You may have more than 9.7 ingredients or fewer for your Secret Sauce Formula for success. I feel a good recipe mix should include at least 3.1 to 9.9 ingredients.

Create your own personal **Secret Sauce Formula**!

The key is to choose daily disciplines and activities that will bring you closer to your goals and dreams in life. These disciplines and activities are what carry you to success. When I help clients create their own personal formula, we go into much greater detail, but I wanted to give you a glimpse of a formula to get you started toward creating your own secret sauce formula for success in life as that will flow over into your success with stock trading and investing as well.

Some possible ingredient suggestions to add to your **Secret Success Formula**, include the following:

> Reading, making bed, jogging, hiking, research, studying, working out, writing, filing, singing, learning a foreign language, typing, walking, cooking, fishing, golf, swimming, think, asking questions, traveling, public speaking, listening to podcasts, watching videos, blogging, personal Bible study, devotional, meeting new people, karate, judo, yoga, meditation, relaxation, painting, drawing, playing piano or guitar or another musical instrument, sewing, knitting, photography, bird watching, gardening, dancing, woodworking, laughing, showing gratefulness, watching comedies

The list of options to put into your "Secret Sauce Formula" mix is endless!

> *An investment in knowledge pays the best interest.*
>
> —Benjamin Franklin

I encourage you to take your self-improvement a step further and incorporate the *quick-charge concept* into your life for greater success and fulfillment.

THE
Quick Charge
CONCEPT
LEARN IT, LIVE IT, INSPIRE OTHERS!

The *Quick Charge Concept* is an approach designed by Tommy Turner that empowers seeking individuals to align their faith and positive mindset with the success and happiness they deserve each and every day.

The Quick Charge Story

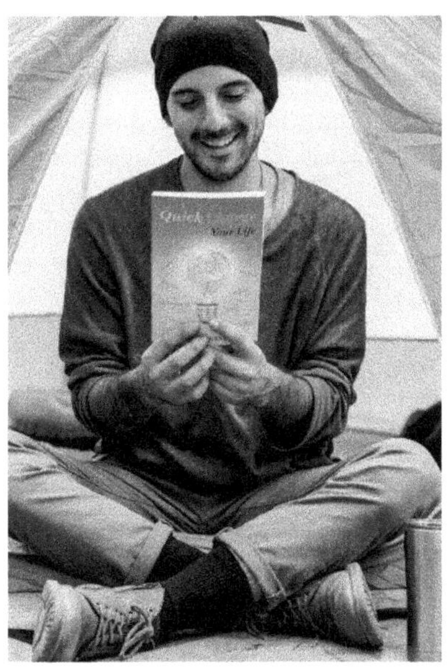

We all have a story. Even the best-intentioned individuals carry with them a past. It's what we do in spite of our setbacks that make us unique. I created the *quick-charge concept* to show you how to derive opportunity out of every single day by making quick, valuable changes that lead to sustained happiness and promising wealth.

I believe within each of us is a manifested dream that is waiting to be realized. I haven't always been a fighter. There was a time when I would let my demons consume me. Anxiety and fear ruled my life for many years. While I wasn't broke, I wasn't thriving the way I had always dreamed I would. Slowly but surely, I figured out a formula for success. For me, turning my life around was only the beginning. By looking inward, I discovered my true calling.

Today, I inspire others to overcome their challenges and achieve the same level of personal and professional success that I have experienced.

The Quick Charge Concept

The *quick-charge concept* delves deep into the authentic energy that grows out of your unique relationship with the Lord. No matter what phase of life you are in, it's never too late to overcome your fears and achieve your true destiny.

I'll help you discover how a positive outlook can help you take responsibility for your happiness—no matter what life throws your way. Together, we'll unlock your ***Secret Sauce Formula*** so that you can achieve your goals and dreams. Once you learn how to live with a positive mindset and complete trust in the Lord's plan, you'll witness the abundance of opportunities before you and feel driven to inspire those around you.

I invite you to let go of the excuses, pain and fear that hold you back so you can engage with the joy right in front of you. God surrounds us with *quick-charge* outlets every day. The time for you to power up and live your life to the fullest is NOW!

> *The quick-charge concept is the proactive way to learn, live and share your dreams.*

Why Quick Charge Your Life?

What is it you want to do in this life? What are the dreams that have yet to come true? If you are tired of falling down and getting back up, I know how you feel. I'll help you take control of your life and experience **happiness**, **wealth**, **freedom**, **peace**, **joy**, **balance** and **confidence** each and every day. Are you living your passion? Every day is an opportunity to give thanks, to be positive, to laugh and to love in the face of anything. Anyone can try to turn a bad day into a good one. The *quick-charge concept* demonstrates that when life hands you lemons, **bite** into them! In this life, there is nothing you cannot overcome. You can climb life's mountain to lasting success and happiness!

Learn it, live it, and inspire others...*Quick Charge Your Life!*

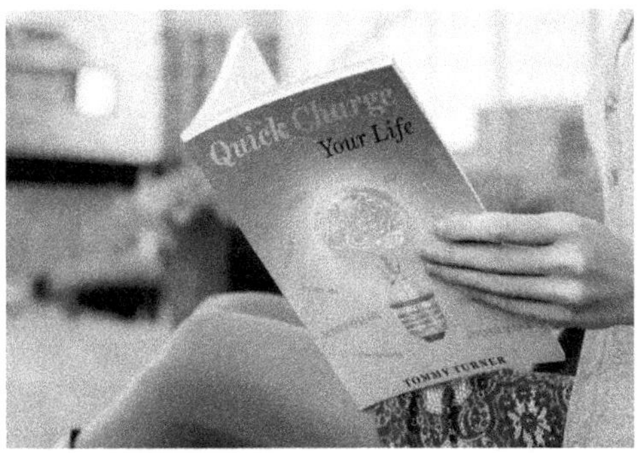

Hire Tommy as Your Personal Investment Coach and Swim With The Sharks!

Why do you need an investment coach? Simple: every industry is filled with subject matter experts whose purpose it is to guide you through the process as painless as possible to help you achieve your goals. Whether it is a professional athlete, author, or investments, there is no safer feeling than knowing someone has your best interests at heart and is willing to work through your difficulties with you as you discover success.

Tommy is a seasoned professional whose mission statement is a mantra of inspiration as he pushes you beyond your perceived limits and step boldly into the life you were born to create. His years of experience and knowledge do the hard work for you. Let's face it, you wouldn't have read this book if you already knew what there was to learn about investing. By hiring Tommy as your coach, you alleviate the constant headaches, misunderstandings, and minimize potential losses. Having an expert in your corner gives you a step above the rest.

The Swim With The Sharks investment coaching program is uniquely designed to go beyond the normal scope of trading and investing in stocks. It is designed to embolden you to find your uniqueness, realize your dreams, and thrive for the rest of your life. Tommy is recognized as one of the best in the business and brings his *quick charge concept* and secret sauce formula to help you achieve greater success in life. Unlike many programs, Tommy shows you how to go beyond just making money. The Swim With The Sharks investment coaching program has strong Christian faith-based roots designed for the believer seeking to elevate their life and investing to the next level.

Are you ready for a fundamental change?

To learn more about the author, Tommy Turner, and the Swim With The Sharks investment coaching program, visit http://tommyturner.com

Quick Charge Your Life Series

For purchasing information about the *Quick Charge* book series, please visit us on the web at http://quickchargeyourlife.com

Tommy Turner's first book simply titled *Quick Charge Your Life* is available on Amazon and Barnes & Noble.

Tuning pianos for many amazing musicians and entertainers over the years, including Johnny Cash, June Carter, Ronnie

Milsap, Lyle Lovett, and JoAnn Castle of "Lawrence Welk" fame, have led to incredible quick-charge moments in Tommy Turner's life. In his first book, *Quick Charge Your Life,* Tommy shares an inspiring encounter with legendary singers, Johnny Cash and his wife June, that forever shaped his life. Discover how *your* daily encounters can forever *quick charge* your life and the lives of those with whom you cross paths...

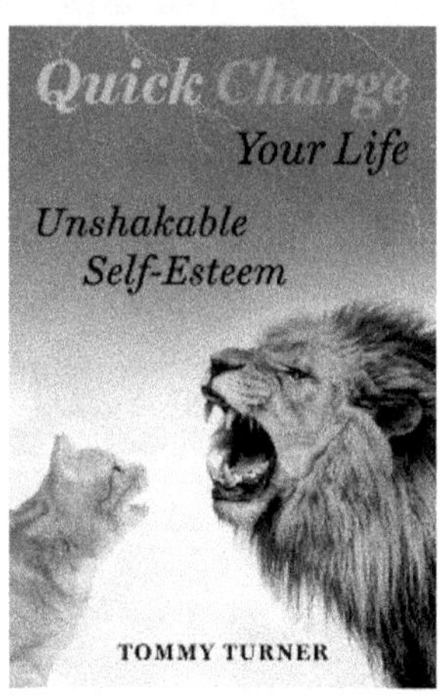

How you VIEW yourself
will either MAKE you or BREAK you.

Developing a quality sense of self-esteem is fundamental to your success. The power of a positive self-esteem can move mountains and produce miracles.

Life will always bring people face to face with unique struggles and hard knocks that threaten to set them back right when they are on the verge of breaking out. That one moment of doubt, that slightest hesitation of questioning will bring their lives to a grinding halt. But what if coming to that standstill didn't need to happen?

All it takes is the proper mindset and no small amount of mental conditioning to awaken our inner resolve and discover the universal truth that we can accomplish anything—with the right amount of confidence and positivity.

Quick Charge Your Life: Unshakable Self-Esteem is the latest installment in the popular *Quick Charge Your Life* series. Each chapter contains a detailed road map to getting and keeping your life on track, healing the fractured parts of your psyche, and learning how to push through the dark times to emerge changed for the better.

Others will notice how YOU feel about yourself and treat you accordingly. Isn't it time to take control of your life and become the person you have always wanted to be? The journey starts with a healthy sense of self-esteem...and this book.

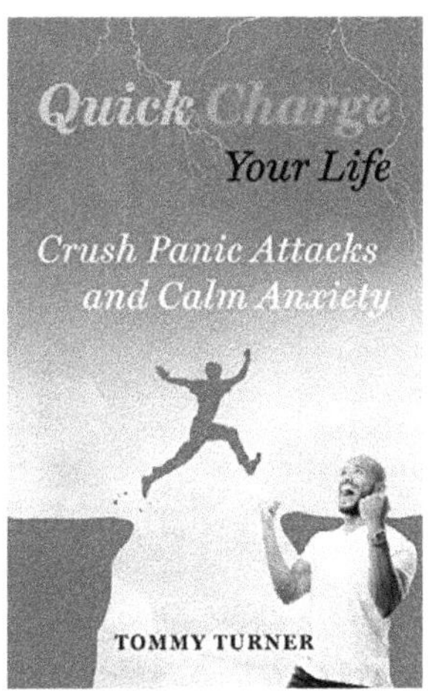

Few things in life can be as crippling and mentally disruptive as panic attacks and anxiety. According to the National Institute of Mental Health up to 7 percent of Americans suffer the debilitating effects of panic disorders. Long-lasting symptoms can reduce our capacity to function. There are six recognized anxiety disorders, each as crippling as the next. The good news is there are multiple ways to combat anxiety and prevent panic attacks before they start.

Quick Charge Your Life: Crush Panic Attacks and Calm Anxiety is written by a man who has dealt with these issues for years in the hopes of showing others how he overcame his demons. This book is a testament to the inner strength we all possess and a way forward for those in need.

No longer do we need to allow fear and anxiety to rule our lives. Each of us dreams of a brighter future, yet not all of us know how to achieve them. *Crush Panic Attacks and Calm Anxiety* is the first step on the path to liberation, and a journey into a beautiful life we all deserve. All it takes is finding the courage to take what is yours.

Contact

For more information about the *quick-charge* book series, please visit us on the web at http://quickchargeyourlife.com. To learn more about the author, Tommy Turner, his coaching programs and courses, visit http://tommyturner.com

www.ingramcontent.com/pod-product-compliance
Lightning Source LLC
Chambersburg PA
CBHW071228210326
41597CB00016B/1986

* 9 7 8 1 9 5 4 2 6 9 0 0 2 *